HOW TECHNOLOGY DEVELOPMENT INFLUENCES ECONOMY GROWTH

JOHN LOK

Contents

Preface

Introduction

What is future (AI) artificial intelligent products development trend and reasonable development stages? How to predict consumer behaviors to persuade who to feel (AI) products are more satisfactory to their needs? Why do consumers feel them to need to buy any (AI) products to use? Will it have other similar products to replace (AI) any products? How is the reasonable stages to achieve future (AI) development in success? Can AI development bring global economic growth or avoid recession? Can future non-manual driving public transport tool inventions bring global economic growth?

In this book, I shall give actual data to predict what the future (AI) products development trend is. Giving my opinions to predict how (AI) consumers' choices are more absolutely. In the (AI) past first stage, I shall concern travel, education, transportation, financial , hospital, administrative service etc. different job natures to indicate how to apply (AI) products to assist these industries more beneficial. In the (AI) nowadays second stage, I shall concentrate on how (AI) developing on education aspect. In the (AI) future third stage, I shall explain why (AI) will have possible to invent (AI) brain technology, even it will bring (AI) war occurence in possible.

In the first (AI) stage, it concerns to be given my opinions to explain how artificial intelligent technology will impact our life and will influence economic development in the future as well as how to influence human job market change. In (AI) labor market stage, I shall indicate how artificial intelligence technology influences future macro global economy change.

In (AI) second stage, I shall indicate how (AI) is developed on education aspect, artificial intelligent technology and online technology and online book stores are high technological intelligent product. Hence, human ourselves will have possible to cause artificial intelligent machine men to own human's mind to learn how to read books and/or write books abilities. When artificial intelligent machine men can learn how to read books and/or write books. Consequently, it means that artificial intelligent machine men can own human mind to do any jobs.I shall assume when artificial intelligent machine men can learn how to write books and/or read books. Then, they will have human's mind ability in possible. Can future artificial intelligent machine men be invented to learn how to write books and/or read books ability? In my this book, I shall attempt to answer this question. Finally, I hope my readers can attempt to make judgement whether artificial intelligent machine men can really learn how to write and/or books. I shall apply online technology to answer this answer. Finally, I shall give my opinions what are the influences when AI machine men had invented to achieve owning human's mind and judgement ability to our future society.

In (AI) third stage development, artificial intelligence (AI) technology is popular to be applied to different industry aspects, such as medical, construction, transportation, hospital, education etc. Although, (AI) is a human invention new development. IN fact, it seems only beneficial to human's daily life. But, it will also have threats to influence human's safety in possible , if some scientists or self-interest mind people who aim to apply (AI) to earn more profit or apply (AI) tools to be weapon to attack other countries to achieve to dominate all human's ambitious intention. Thus, (AI) will bring negative influences to our society, instead of positive influences if we can not apply this kind of new technological tools immorally. In this stage, I shall give my opinions to indicate what reasons will cause (AI) artificial intelligent tools to be applied to social military defense weapon by human's intention. In my this books, I hope my readers can know what will cause human's immoral behaviors to bring our societies to bring more dangerous or risks or threats if human applied (AI) technology to achieve whose immoral or ambitious intention. Finally, I hope that human ought not apply (AI) technology to do any behavioral attack to satisfy ourselves interest or dominate global world ambition to avoid (AI) technological war occurrence in the future one day.

In (AI) fourth stage, I shall give some university lecturers' personal analytical mind to judge whether what will be occurred if artificial intelligence could be invented to match to own human brain's mind ability? What will be the advantages and/or disadvantages if (AI) robots would be invented to match to own human brain's mind ability?

I shall follow current (AI) technological development to judge whether what the potential abilities are that (AI) will achieve to satisfy human's life needs when (AI) is invented to own human brain in future one day.

In future stage, we are experiencing technological development stages, human began to consider air pollution how brings our natural environment to cause worse. Our cars fuel emission can also pollute our air when we are often driving ourselves cars to go to anywhere for leisure or working aim. Instead of ourselves cars emission air pollution, public transport tools, such as buses, taxis, ferries, their fuel emission also influence our air to be polluted. Because passenger individual comfort need began raises. So, electric auto non-manual driving cars, battery charge energy cars are began to consider how to invent in order to reduce air pollution and raise driver individual comfortable need, instead of improving driving speed to be rapid, car inventors also hope to avoid air pollution to pollute our natural environment. When global fuel cars number continues increases. How man made clever automobile may well engage clever transportation tools ? Can man made intelligence (AI) and laptop studying (ML) be utilized in the quest for brand spanking new " intake" behavioral kind variables that have an effect on purchaser person or transportation carrier association person diverse transportation instruments offerings, corresponding to street or sea or sky transportation instruments? Can man made clever car might engage clever transportation instruments industry development?

This road transport part brings readers to image what will be different if artificial intelligent non manual driving vehicle will be used to public transportation and private transportation both aspects in popular. Will it popular to accept to use any artificial intelligent vehicles? Is it possible to apply AI non-manual driving technology to AI non-manual driving transportation tools global transportation market? For example, in (AI) non-manual vehicle industry, driving automatic vehicle whether it will be accepted to drivers who have confidence to drive it on roads safely. Whether artificial (AI) intelligent non-manual driving systems are the improvement of traffic safety, reduction of energy consumption or improvement of the comfort of the driver. Whether will it be popular to accept to apply artificial intelligent non-manual driving technology from non-manual auto driving cars to be applied to any non-manual auto driving transportation tools transportation market development, such as train, tram, lorry, transportation air plane, passenger air plane, ferry, taxi, MTR. Etc. different kinds of transportation tools? If future human accepts to use any non-manual driving vehicles or non-manual driving transportation tools, what advantages and disadvantages will bring to influence our daily life.

How if (AI) non-manual auto driving technology stage is mature to achieve non-manual driving technology is safe driving. It is possible that (AI) non-manual driving cars can influence to change whole manual driving transportation tools to non-manual driving transportation tools. How it will influence (AI) autonomous cars change to influence global manual driving transportation industry development ? To achieve non-manual driving industry development success. (AI) non-manual driving vehicle manufacturers need to ensure (AI) driving system is more safe to drive to compare manual driving on the road. If they expect non-manual driving transportation market development success. So, self improving systems are a promising new approach to developing artificial intelligence. But will their behavior be predictable? Can will be sure that they will behave as we intended even after many generations of self improvement? This part presents a framework for answering any questions concern whether future non-manual driving transportation market whether it will be possible to bring global economic growth in success.

Prologue

Table of contents

The influences when AI is invented to own human's mind and judgement abilities

Artificial intelligence and the future of defense or teaching choice

Online technology and online book technology influences artificial intelligence mind development

Prediction of artificial intelligence
reading and writing abilities

development

The influences when AI is invented to own human's mind and judgement abilities

Why does AI machine lecturer can raise education quality?

Future AI machine education market
- (AI) university lecture assistant
- (AI) secondary and primary teacher assistant
- (AI) scientific research assistant

Artificia intelligent future education market development
Artificial intelligent robots invention negative impacts
Future AI tutoring system potential development market
How can potential social teaching robots assist to teacher in school?
Psychological research (AI) eduational social robots and students relationship

economic growth
Can AI avoids economic recession p.88-9

CHAPTER I

Competitive influences between artificial intelligence and human job

Although, (AI) technology will be popular to applied to different jobs, but it still needs social acceptance to replace some human jobs. Today, it is increasingly common for people to use robots in various situations at home and in retail stores, hotels and hospitals. Robots are classified into several types based on their functionality (service and utility robots or those designed to communicate with humans) and appearance (humanoid robots or mechanical robots). The types of robot to which every country attaches particular important in the advance of robotics, reflects the sense of values and preferences of its population . Thus, (AI) will be applied to replace human to do these above different kinds of job nature. For example, U.S. has the highest level of robot utilization at home and an retail stores with its people being the most enthusiastic about the future use of robots. Otherwise, Germany shows a strong tendency to consider robots for industrial purposes, and its people feel strong to the presence of robots in their households. Japanese accepts to apply" human aid robot" that can communicate with humans and they have a high level of familiarity with robots.

Hence, it implied those three countries have accept (AI) to replace human to do any these kinds of job duty and it will influence these three countries' workers lose their old occupations and who will unemployed absolutely, due to many (AI) robots replace them to do their job duties in the future. Also, US will have many retail service workers or retail warehouse workers are unemployed. Germany will have many manufacturing industry's workers are unemployed. Japanese will have many communication industry workers are unemployed, such as telephone service, shopping center services etc. different kind of service industry's service staffs . It will cause these kind of workers' competitive abilities are lost in themselves countries' jobs that require such skills include software developers, court judges, nurses, high school teachers, dentists and university lecturers, these occupations are still difficult to be replaced by

(AI) robots.

Are robots taking our jobs or making them? In fact, our societies will have unemployment challenges, even (AI) technology has not created before. However, after (AI) robots invention, some of human jobs will be replaced and it can raise many low skillful and low knowledge level worker unemployment number. However, I think that high productivity driven by increasingly powerful IT -enabled machines is the causes of global labor market problems and accelerating technological change will only make those problems worse.

IT technology brings this question: Are robots killing human's jobs or benefiting human's jobs? I suppose that there is a limited amount of labor to be done. The implication is that technology can create unemployment by displacing workers, such as (AI) invention, because the more efficiently worker work (using machines or (AI) robots), the loss work there is for workers to do. Even, any new jobs will be better done by machines or (AI) robots, and unemployment will still skyrocket. How do we know that humans will always be better at some work, or more importantly, enough work, than machines or (AI) robots, e.g. human drivers drive more safe or careful to compare (AI) robot drivers. But, the challenge is that it is not ensure that (AI) robots drivers must not drive careless to cause the chance of accident occurrences more than human drivers. However, technological change can be beneficial to innovation, automation and increasing productivity for businesses.

Consequently , it may seem machines can hurt wages and job for low skillful, less educated workers. Also, high educated workers are likely as less educated workers to find themselves displaced and devalued, and more education may create as many problems as it solves. Thus, in negative influence, automation effects on particular jobs shift workers to other jobs that are equally or more desirable. Workers may be highly compensated for possessing human capital that is specialized to a labor market. If technological advance is very rapid, such as (AI) invention, causing a large and very rapid drop in demand in a large labor market, the economy may not be able to absorb the sudden surplus of labor in a short period of timer when (AI) robots are popular to replace some workers to do some occupations in global societies.

For example, self-driving vehicles threaten to send truck drivers to the unemployment office. Computer programs can now write journalistic accounts of sporting events and stock price movement. There are even computers that can grade essay revolutionize some part of teaching jobs. Hence, (AI) robots will have possible to replace human brain to do any judgement, argument, and mind job duties. It implies some occupations which need human' mind will be threaten by (AI) robots, e.g. author, accountant, nurse, engineer. Thus, (AI) robots will have possible to replace some professional and high educated workers' jobs in the future.

But, technology can create new nature of jobs in possible. For example, a 60 minutes program indicated technology is putting new categories of jobs in the sites (sic) of automation, the 60% of the workforce that makes its living gathering and analyzing information. Also, recession: technology kills middle -class jobs that overall technology is eliminating for more jobs than it is creating by (AI) technology. Hence, human's brain work may be assisted by 60% of (AI) gathering and analyzing information for some occupation , e.g. space scientists, ocean scientists, earth scientists etc.

However, I believe the (AI) invention and human job competition may influence global productivity change. Productivity is economic output per unit of input, the unit of on input can be labor hours(labor productivity), but if (AI) robots replace human job, then the unit of input may be (AI) machine hours (AI) robot productivity or all production factors including labors, machines and energy (total factor of productivity). Producing more output with less input can take several forms.

The traditional notion of productivity is a form reorganizing production and/or using better or more technology to produce more output per worker hour. But when (AI) robots invention, the form can be reorganizing production and/or using better or more (AI) robots to produce more output per (AI) robot hour. Hence, if the firm apply (AI) robots to produce its products. Then , productivity improvements in the firm may result in less workers employment, due to (AI) robots replace more worker number to achieve more productivity improvement, it has economic benefits (less factor of production) , but more production in long term.

Thus, (AI) robots can help any firm to achieve productivity improvement in long term, for example, if unproductve farmers move to the city and start working for high-tech. manufacturers. The shift effect can be more dynamic and disruptive as low-productivity industries lose out in the marketplace to high -productivity industries and the compositional mix of the economy changes. Thus, in the long term (AI) robots can also be beneficial to high productivity industries to bring the mix of economy positive changes.

Moreover, automation will also produce some new jobs in firms that sell the new robot or other labor-saving technology. This means that, in general, there will be shift in the economy in the direction of higher-skill and higher wage jobs. Even if the (AI) robot invention country, US becomes a leader in (AI) robots producing productivity-enhancing technology, it will experience a growth in jobs serving foreign (AI) robots product buyers. Hence, (AI) robots can also create (AI) salespeople, (AI) manufacturing workers , (AI) inventors, scientists, (AI) software designer etc. occupations, when if all society does is move workers from insurance firms, restaurants and car factories to robot factories, productivity will have remained the same to create job needs for insurance, restaurant and car manufacturing worker service occupations for (AI) software designer, (AI) service robots manufacturer, (AI) service robot seller etc. related (AI) service robot product occupation created in (AI) robot technology job market. Hence, (AI) invention also create new (AI) technology job chance. (AI) impacts management job market.

In future, organization management will be changed from (AI) introduction. Division of labor will change and collaboration among humans and machines will increase. Companies will have to adapt their training, performance and talent acquisition strategies to account for a new found emphasis on work that hinges on human
judgement and skills, including experimentation and colloboration.

How (AI) impacts any organizational administrative management work? (AI) 's greatest impact will be on administrative coordination and control tasks, such as scheduling, resource allocation and reporting, (AI)-driven will place a higher premium on what we call " judgement work", the application of human experience and expertise to critical business decisions and practices when information available is insufficient to suggest a successful course of action. This kind of work will require new skills and mindsets; replacing people with machines is not goal in itself. When, artificial intelligence enables cost-cutting automation of routine work, it also empowers value -adding augmentation of human capabilities.

Thus, administrative and routine tasks, such as scheduling, allocation of resources, and reporting, will within intelligent machines, responsibilities that have long been reserved for humans. For instance, a typical store manager or a lead nurse at a nursing home must constantly juggle shift schedules, accounting for staff members' absense owing to illness, vaction, time or sudden departures. Many of these tasks will be automated by (AI).

Imagine (AI) writing management monthly reports, it is not a distant dream. Leading news providers and Wall street banks are now using (AI) report generators to write news and analytical reports by drawing on quantitative data. The associated press, for example, expanded its quarterly earnings reporting from approximately 300 companies to nearly 3,000 with the help of (AI) powered software robots, freeing up journalists to conduct more investigative and interpretive reporting. For another example, Jobalime, a job-placement site, uses intelligent voile analysis algorithms to evaluate job applicants. The algorithm assesses paralinguistic elements of speech, such as tone and inflection, products which emotions a specific voice will elicit, and identifies the type of work at which an applicant will likely excel. In the future , (AI) machines can be applied to assist some kind of office administrative jobs duties. It's attractive to office managers to achieve more accurate judgment to do any administrative matters when who can be assisted from (AI) machines. Thus, managers need to spend time to learn how to apply (AI) machine to assist them to do more accurate judgement, and better informed choices. (AI) robots can be applied to improve the speed quality and cost of available products and services, instead of applying on productivity improvement and administrative improvement aspects. Thus, they may also displace large numbers of workers. This, possibility challenges the traditional benefits model of trying health care and retirement savings to jobs.

In an economy that employs dramatically fewer workers to deliver benefits to displaced workers. For example, the worldwide number of industrial robots has increased rapidly over the past few years. The fall prices of robots, which can operate all day without interruption, make them cost- competitive with human workers. In special consideration, in the service sector, computer algorithums can execute stock trades in a fraction of a second, much faster than any human. As those technologies become cheaper, more capable, and more widespread, they will find even more applicants in an economy.

Consequently, (AI) technology brings unemployed number increasing many businesses continued automating their operations rather than hiring additional workers. A trend among technology companies that receive massive valuations with relatively few workers. For example, in 2014 year Google was valued at $370 billion with only 55,000 employees, a tenth the size of AT & T's workforce in the 1960 year. Hence, if automation technologies like robots and artificial intelligence make jobs less secure in the future, there needs to be a way to deliver benefits outside of employment " flexi security" or flexible security is one idea for providing healthcare, education and housing assistance whether or not someone is formally employed.

In conclusion, (AI) and robots technology will raise unemployment to some occupations when (AI) replaces same industries' workers job duties in our societies in the future, but it also create new jobs to raise employment in any related (AI) robots and automated machine products in (AI) manufacturing. (AI) design, (AI) sale self-related industry, when (AI) replaces same industries' workers' job duties.

How artificial intelligence replaces human job possibility

What is the risk of automation for jobs to replace human job? In recent years, there has been a revival of concerns that automation and digitalization night after all result in jobless future. As I argue, this might lead to an overestimation of job (AI) automate , as occupations labelled as high-risk occupations often still contain a substantial share of tasks that are hard to automate.

For example, when the share of (AI) automatable jobs is 6% in Korea, the corresponding share is 12% in Australia. Differences between countries may reflect general differences in workplace organization, differences in previous investments into (AI) automation technologies as well as differences in the education of workers across countries. I also discover that (AI) automation and digitalization are unlikely to destroy large numbers of jobs. But, however, low qualified labors are likely to raise costs as the (AI) automate of their jobs is higher compared to highly qualified workers.

In fact, (AI) technology will influence some new technology to replace some human's job, such as driverless car, the largely autonomous smart factory , service robots or 3D printing. These technologies are driven by advances in computing power, robotics and artificial intelligence and ultimately redefine what type of human capabilities machines are able to do.

Hence, question brings whether (AI) invention will influence general human jobs to be replaced by (AI) autonomous jobs? Whether will the potential foe automation with actual employment loss? In particular, the technical possibility to use (AI) machines rather tasks need not mean that the substitution of humans by machines actually takes place.

Whether (AI) technology replaces human's some job, it is beneficial to our society or not. Instead, machines are increasingly capable of performing non-routine cognitive tasks, such as driving or legal writing . In particular, advances in the field of machine learning (ML), e.g. computational statistics and visions, data mining, artificial intelligences allow for automating cognitive task, when the use of (ML) in mobile robotics (MR) also allows for automating certain manual tasks. So, it seems, (AI) technology can replace some labor job, e.g. warehouse transportation, even mind's job, e.g. legal writing, driving in possible.

For example, if (AI) automatic non-manual driving can reduce hurt or death risk, it is beneficial to our society, or (AI) automatic robots can more any heavy things (products) in warehouse safely. Then, it can reduce the warehouse labor's bodies hour risk, it is beneficial to the workers. Even, if (AI) robot can write any legal documents, no any word errors in short time. It is beneficial to the law companies , but it also bring unemployment chance, due to these jobs can be replaced by (AI) robots to do in the future. Hence, it will cause some occupation to be disappeared, due to (AI) robots can do our these kinds of jobs in the future.

Frey & Osborne (2013) reported these kinds of occupations will be replaced by (AI) robots in possible. They include computer, engineering, financial, management, legal , art and medium, community service, education, healthcare practitioners and technical service, sales and related, office and administrative support, farming, fishing and forestry, construction and extraction, installation, maintenance, and repair , production, transportation and material moving. It seems our future some professional occupations will have possible to the replaced by (AI) robots to replace, instead of labor jobs. Hence, (AI) robots technology will have much trend to replace high knowledge or low knowledge skillful labors in the future.

In conclusion, it implies that only using information on task-usage at the individual level leads to significantly lower estimates of jobs " at risk", some workers in occupations with according to high automate nevertheless often perform tasks with are hard to automate. Why can (AI) replace human to do some kinds of jobs? (AI) artificial intelligence refers to the ability of a computer or a computer enable robotic system to process information and produce outcomes in a manner similar to the thought process of humans in learning, decision making and solving problem. By extension, the goal of (AI) systems is to develop systems to capable of tasking complex problems in ways similar to human's logic and reasons who feel in our future. Hence, it means future (AI) robots has effort to replace human to do any jobs in possible.

CHAPTER II

(AI) journalism, media publishing, digital communication technology trend

How to apply (AI) technology in digital communication journalism media, publishing industry? Some scientists indicate future (AI) and digital technology may consist such as: voice driven assistants, emerge. For example, Amazon e book publish applying digital technology and (AI) auto printing technology to sell e books to let readers to listen any e book content by (AI) voice driven speaker when they turn on computer to read e book contents; capable phones start to unlock the possibilities of 3D image of mobile story telling. New smart wearables include ear buds that handle instant translation and glasses that talk and hear. China and India will become a key focus for digital growth with innovations around payment online identity, and artificial intelligence. Thus, future (AI) technology can be applied to 3D image mobile story telling, online payment method to dealt online transaction publishing industry.

Thus, future (AI) technology can be applied to online e book publishing industry to make sound books to let readers feel more attractive . Such as Amazon publish has published sound e books to attract readers to choose to read any its books from online. Also, (AI) technology can also be applied to communication industry. For example, some online pure-play news, opinion and entertainment websites. It is a digital communication media, e.g. online journalism blog (AI) technology can be applied to visual storytellers to let online book readers to enjoy to listen to watch and send any online electronic book contents more attractive. Thus, future (AI) technology will be popular to assist any electronic book publishers to publish visual and sound talking storybook to let readers who can watch motive image and listen and read words from e books more attractive.

Thus, (AI) technology can be applied to internet ecommerce publishing or media industry to help any electronic book publishers to publish sound, image motion electronic book to attract global readers to read, even (AI) technology can be applied to digital entertainment industry, e.g. electronic 3D image virtual video games, computer games. It can be also applied to education industry, e.g. the first true digital native generation and are the native speakers of the digital language of computers to let student to learn different languages or translate words to compare to classroom learning more easily. It can be also applied to communication industry, e.g. (AI) mobile phone. Hence, it seems (AI) technology can be applied to publishing, communication, education , entertainment etc. different industries in the future. (AI) technology will be one kind of tool to satisfy human's daily life needs in the future and these industries has one characteristics is that they need to apply internet to operate to operate to do online business.

Thus, it has three trends of (AI) technology and internet technology need to be linked to achieve one kind of attractive technological business to satisfy client's needs. These three trends as below: All consumer trends involve the internet. It will be many consumer's online habits, shopping, working, socializing, watching TV, studying, travelling, listening. Thus, (AI) music, eating and exercising are just a few examples. This is happening because human usually use mobile broadband or Wi-Fi, rather than cables. Thus, (AI) technology will be applied to mobile to satisfy client's need absolutely.

The mobile phone can be more popular to be used more than computer or laptop tools. The reasons are because women dive the smartphone market by defining mass-market use. But as the speed of technology adoption increases mass market use becomes much quicker then before. Successful new technological products and services , such a (AI) mobile phone products now reach the mass market in popular use. It means that the time period when early adopters influence others is shorter than before. Also, since new products and services increasingly use the internet mass markets are not only faster , but are also more important than ever to consumer themselves. Most internet services become more valuable to individuals when many use them. Thus, it causes why (AI) mobile phone will be popular to be used.

Since, new products and services increasingly use the internet, in the future several trends focus on (AI) smart phone users. Consumers' familiarity with using smartphone apps. Essentially, the technologies will bring other related (AI) and internet service needs, e.g. sound and image emotion e book needs, (AI) mobile communication needs, e-virtual games or e-3D image virtual games etc. entertainment activities needs with such a large part of the world's population now online, it is clear that there is strength in numbers.

Thus, (AI) imagines , if future any (AI) and internet related services or products new technology is easy to use and inexpensive, when the latest products reach the mass market almost as quickly as they reach the early adopters and industry experts. I believe that any (AI) and internet related products or services must be popular to accept to consume for entertainment or useful aim. For example, with major players including Apply, Facebook and Google had invested (AI) technology to develop their businesses. (AI) technology has the potential to disrupt everything in the coming years, from the lives of connected consumers to every industry (AI) will be an alternative route for brands to reach consumers with convincing and relevant messages. Digital technology will assist of the future, then it can improve technology to bring this effect, such as sophisticated software machine learning and speech recognition effective. Hence, Google, Facebook , Yahoo web site service companies can apply (AI) technology to help other companies to advertise their businesses, such as travel, retail, and education etc. industries more attractive. (AI) technology can be applied to internet company to be aware and familiar enough to drive among mainstream consumers, it can create online experience to travel, retail , education and other entertainment needs to online consumers to seek their entertainment needs more easily. Hence, in the future (AI) technology and internet related entertainment service needs will be raised in this (AI) and online consumption market.

- (AI) healthcare service industry development

In the future, (AI) medical internet technology tool can be applied to assist individual's health at the center of their focus, e.g. smartwatch compatible mobile app. patients can let personalized reminders for taking their medication snap pictures of their prescriptions to expedite refills, and scan their insurance card. So that, store clerks are prepared with up-to-date patients' information . (AI) owned health operated technological clinics can help patients to receive treatment for minor illnesses, flu shots, cholesterol screenings and more than a dozen other medical services, all of which can be patients who can't make it to a physical location. (AI) healthcare services organizations can provide various telemedicine services. So, patients can receive care via phone or video chat.

For example, one London-based intelligent Brewing company has developed an (AI) system to continuously collect and incorporate customer feedback, which the system itself uses to brew ne various of the company's beers. Thus, the beer clients can give feedback to talk to the algorithm (AI) machine, whenever or anywhere who're drinking the beer. It is such any healthcare services organizations can apply (AI) machine to collect patient's feedback to talk to the algorithum (AI) machine whenever or anywhere who're eating any medicines. So doctors can know every patient's health conditions any time. If the patients feel uncomfortable, the doctor can know from (AI) machine notification to decide whether the patient needs to eat another new medicine or keep to eat same medicine is better. Hence, (AI) medial internet technological body check report machine will be proper to be needed to serve any hospitals' patients in the future.

However , it brings this question. How can (AI) medical internet technological body check report machine apply to hospital more efficient? The essential new medicine co-workers for the health service digital age health service leaders need apply (AI) medical report machines and artificial intelligence to the newest recruits to the workforce bringing new skills to help health service staffs do new jobs and reinventing what's possible, building the health service workforce for today's digital health service demands for patients. Thus, technology-driven health service model innovation from the health service organization outside in and providing digital health service ecosystems for patients to use the (AI) health service equipment will be popular to be accepted to be used.

- I Robot and internet things future machine men invention

Nowadays, there are some company, which apply internet and (AI) I Robot technology to do any similar human job nature. For fishing industry example, one company, known for creating the Roomba, I Robot is now working with marine conservationists to launch an ocean-patrolling intelligent robot to hunt and manage invasive species, protecting native populations. And evolved industries like precision agriculture are ramping of our increasing population. Area of practice that once seemed impossible to digitize are fundamentally changing because of the impacts of (AI), internet of things capabilities and big data analytics, which have many potentially positive impactions for society.

For textile industry example, automation is nothing new, it has shaped the workplace to replace human jobs to boost productivity in the textile industry. Textile machines have had a generally positive impact over gears, creating value and allowing textile workers to take up more rewarding age will likely continue to create opportunities and lead to new textile industries, companies and textile occupations. It may also compensate for a demographically driven slowdown in the growth of the textile workforce. The future impact of textile (AI) and automatic and internet link is somewhat uncertain. It seems textile industry will be trend to accept (AI) textile workers and internet of thing to replace traditional manual textile workers to produce any shirts, cloths etc. wearing products in factories popularly, during the (AI) textile machine and internet thing technology can be invented to reach the mature stage in the future.

For factory worker transportation job example, they have also expanded their influence, migrating from the factory floor to the service sector and taking the place of humans in a range of activities from financial transactions to transport route optimization. Further (AI) machines and robots are increasingly programmed to learn, meaning they improve with time and undertake cognitive activities. Hence, (AI) machines and internet technology enable automation of work activities to raise factory workers' efficient and performances, also factories can reduce manual worker numbers, due to (AI) machine workers' assistance.

Future, (AI) robotics technologies and internet technique have these different kinds of characteristics: For soft robotics example, it is non-rigid robots construct with soft and deformable materials that can manipulate items of varying size, shape and weight with a single device. For swarm robotics, it coordinated multi-robot systems often involving large numbers of mostly physical robots. For touch/factile robotic example, it robotic body pails (often biologically inspired hands) with capability to sense, touch , dexterity robots example, serpentine robots with many internal degrees of freedom to threat through tightly packed spaces for humanoid robots example, robots physical is similar to human being often bi-pedal that investigate variety capable of performing human tasks , including movement across terrains, object recognition, speech sensing etc. For autonomous cars and trucks example, it is capable of operating with a human pilot, e.g. the unarmed general atomics Predator XPUAV with roughly half the wingspan of a Boeing 737 can fly autonomously for up to 35 hours from take-off to landing, for unmanned aerial vehicles example, flying vehicles capable of operating without a human pilot, the unarmed general atomics predator -XPUAV , with roughly half thc wingspan of a Boing 737, and fly autonomously for up to 35 hours from take off to landing, for (AI) chat bots example, (AI) systems designed to simulate conversation with human users, particularly those integrated into massaging apps.

In Dec. 2015. the general service administration of the US Govt. described how it used a chat bot named Mrs. Landingham (a character from the television show the west wing) to help onboard new employees. Finally, for robotic process automation example, class of software robots that replicates the actions of a human being interacting with the user interfaces of both software systems. Enables the automation of many back-office work flows without requiring expensive IT integration . Hence, future (AI) robot machine men will have different functions to be applied to different industries to use in possible.

Statistics Denmark shows that (AI) automation potential robots will influence few jobs are completely automatable , but close to half consists of 40% automatable tasks: It showed example occupations include share of automated, such as brewing machine operators are more than 80%, logging equipment operators are more than 50%, roofers , stock tasks clerks, travel agent are more than 50%, farmers , nursing assistants are more than 30%, physicians, teachers , managers are more than 10%.

For example, humans perform a wide variety of tasks from planting corn to examine spreadsheets, meeting clients and lifting crates in a store. Each of these actions requires a combination of innate or acquired capabilities, internet technique assistance, ranging from social perceptiveness to fine motor skills and natural language understanding. To understand and map automation feasibility by existing technology. Mc Kinsey has developed a framework of 18 technical capabilities that can substitute tasks performed by humans. The capabilities are grouped in five categories: sensory, cognitive, language, social and emotional and physical. So, it seems (AI) robot machine men and internet technique will have possible combination to invent to own human's emotion , language, learning, task skill abilities.

Mckinsey global institute analysis also showed current technologies have achieved different levels of human performance across 18 capabilities include: sensory perception, autonomously infer and integrate complex input using sensors, cognitive capabilities reorganizing known patterns/ categories supervised learnings, generating novel, logical reasoning/ problem solving, optimization and planning, creative, information retrieval, coordination with multiple agents, output articulation/presentation, national language processing, social and emotional capabilities-natural language understanding, social and emotion sense, reasoning output, physical capabilities-fine motor skills, navigation mobility. Hence, it seems (AI) robots and internet technological will combine to invent to own human' some skills to replace human to do some kind of tasks in possible.

In conclusion, future (AI) robot and internet will be needed to link to cooperate together to raise human's work efficiency in popular.

How artificial intelligence replaces human job possibility

What is the risk of automation for jobs to replace human job? In recent years, there has been a revival of concerns that automation and digitalization night after all result in jobless future. As I argue, this might lead to an overestimation of job (AI) automate , as occupations labelled as high-risk occupations often still contain a substantial share of tasks that are hard to automate.

For example, when the share of (AI) automatable jobs is 6% in Korea, the corresponding share is 12% in Australia. Differences between countries may reflect general differences in workplace organization, differences in previous investments into (AI) automation technologies as well as differences in the education of workers across countries. I also discover that (AI) automation and digitalization are unlikely to destroy large numbers of jobs. But, however, low qualified labors are likely to raise costs as the (AI) automate of their jobs is higher compared to highly qualified workers.

In fact, (AI) technology will influence some new technology to replace some human's job, such as driverless car, the largely autonomous smart factory , service robots or 3D printing. These technologies are driven by advances in computing power, robotics and artificial intelligence and ultimately redefine what type of human capabilities machines are able to do.

Hence, question brings whether (AI) invention will influence general human jobs to be replaced by (AI) autonomous jobs? Whether will the potential foe automation with actual employment loss? In particular, the technical possibility to use (AI) machines rather tasks need not mean that the substitution of humans by machines actually takes place.

Whether (AI) technology replaces human's some job, it is beneficial to our society or not. Instead, machines are increasingly capable of performing non-routine cognitive tasks, such as driving or legal writing . In particular, advances in the field of machine learning (ML), e.g. computational statistics and visions, data mining, artificial intelligences allow for automating cognitive task, when the use of (ML) in mobile robotics (MR) also allows for automating certain manual tasks. So, it seems, (AI) technology can replace some labor job, e.g. warehouse transportation, even mind's job, e.g. legal writing, driving in possible.

For example, if (AI) automatic non-manual driving can reduce hurt or death risk, it is beneficial to our society, or (AI) automatic robots can more any heavy things (products) in warehouse safely. Then, it can reduce the warehouse labor's bodies hour risk, it is beneficial to the workers. Even, if (AI) robot can write any legal documents, no any word errors in short time. It is beneficial to the law companies , but it also bring unemployment chance, due to these jobs can be replaced by (AI) robots to do in the future. Hence, it will cause some occupation to be disappeared, due to (AI) robots can do our these kinds of jobs in the future.

Frey & Osborne (2013) reported these kinds of occupations will be replaced by (AI) robots in possible. They include computer, engineering, financial, management, legal , art and medium, community service, education, healthcare practitioners and technical service, sales and related, office and administrative support, farming, fishing and forestry, construction and extraction, installation, maintenance, and repair , production, transportation and material moving. It seems our future some professional occupations will have possible to the replaced by (AI) robots to replace, instead of labor jobs. Hence, (AI) robots technology will have much trend to replace high knowledge or low knowledge skillful labors in the future.

In conclusion, it implies that only using information on task-usage at the individual level leads to significantly lower estimates of jobs " at risk", some workers in occupations with according to high automate nevertheless often perform tasks with are hard to automate. Why can (AI) replace human to do some kinds of jobs? (AI) artificial intelligence refers to the ability of a computer or a computer enable robotic system to process information and produce outcomes in a manner similar to the thought process of humans in learning, decision making and solving problem. By extension, the goal of (AI) systems is to develop systems to capable of tasking complex problems in ways similar to human's logic and reasons who feel in our future. Hence, it means future (AI) robots has effort to replace human to do any jobs in possible.

CHAPTER III

(AI) directions for future non-manual control road vehicles market

Future road vehicle products and technologies must meet social, economic and environmental protection and driving safety goals , and satisfying market requirements for mobility, accident reducing, performance, cost desirability. Thus, (AI) auto-non manual control vehicles need to be followed this direction to invent. To satisfy future driver's safety of needs, enhanced vehicle speed desired functional performance of road transportation system, required and desired technological response, including research needs. It is long term up to 20 years vision, for (AI) auto non-manual research. Thus, (AI) auto non manual vehicle manufacturers need often to revise their (AI) vehicles functions to raise to improve their system performance and driving industry driver's needs, e.g. private drivers need or public transportation driver's need or business client's need. Hence, future (AI) transportation will need have individual driving consumer and business driving consumer both targets.

Thus, future (AI) automation manual control vehicles need to deliver high impact technology solutions to meet social , economic and environmental and safe goals. Engine needs to be improved efficiency , performance, drivability, reliability, durability and speed-to-market together with reduced emissions and cost; hybrid, electric and alternatively fuel (AI) non manual control vehicle technology development, leading to new fuel and power systems, such as hydrogen, fuel cells and batteries, which satisfy future social, economic and environmental and safe goals. Software, sensors, electronics and telematics technology development are needed to be lead to improve vehicle performance, control and adaptability, intelligent , mobility and security, structure and materials technology development, leading to improved safety, performance and leading to flexibility with reduced cost and environmental pollution to achieve the (AI) non manual drivers to feel (AI) vehicle performance, auto control and adaptability is better to compare traditional manual driving vehicles.

In fact, in traditional manual driving market, Japan and USA had had over 80% of world car production by six major global groups. In the future, it is possible only USA can dominate (AI) non manual auto driving vehicle manufacturing market if Japan had no effort to manufacture any (AI) auto non manual control vehicles. So, it means that it is only Japan is USA potential (AI) auto non manual control vehicle manufacturing competitors. Also, it means that it is only USA has effort to export (AI) auto non manual control vehicles to global (AI) auto non manual control vehicle market.

Thus, in long term, (AI) non manual control vehicle product market development, USA (AI) vehicle manufacturers will have these requirement to win new technological competition to traditional manual control vehicle. The requirements include: low cost fuel, low carbon, fuel cell and telematics technologies, the technological roadmap function, such as detailed consideration clear provision of other important areas to the drivers. When the (AI) non manual auto drivers are sitting in the non manual control auto vehicle. Although, who does not need to drive, but who need to know how to go to anywhere by electric road map show clearly. So, the driver won't lose direction and he/she can know the (AI) non manual control vehicles is driving to anywhere in any time, even when who is sleeping.

In the future, the (AI) non manual control vehicles need to be invented to satisfy any business , transportation clients' needs, instead of individual clients needs, e.g. cans, trucks, buses, emergency and utility vehicles, trains, trams etc. Hence, technological road mapping is one important tool to help any business, transportation (AI) non manual control vehicle clients. Technological roadmap is a technique that is used in industry to support strategic planning for (AI) non manual driving vehicles in the future. Electronic road maps generally take the form of multi-layered time based charts, linking technology developments to future (AI) non manual control vehicle market requirements.

Technology road mapping is a flexible technique and the roadmap architecture and process for developing the roadmap most generally be customized to meeting the particular aims. Why technology roadmap will be popular to (AI_ non manual control vehicles. It's advantages include: It is a technology solutions and options that can enable the performance targets to be achieved engine hybrid, electric and alternatively fueled vehicles, software, sensors electronics and telematics, structures and materials design and manufacturing process. It is road transport system performance measures and targets tool, in response to the trends and get (AI) non manual control vehicle drivers to get society, economy, environment protection, low cost driving benefits, also it can help any transportation clients to know how to go to anywhere clearly. Hence, technological road map will be one good tool to assist (AI) non manual control auto vehicle to develop future road driving market.

Reference(source)

Frey & Osborne (2013), The future of employment: How susceptible are jobs to computerization? University of Oxford.

Mckinsey Global Institute Analysis

Statistics Denmark, Global automation impact model, Makinsey analysis

(AI) development second stage

Chapter Five (AI) -driven automation industry development

(AI) -driven automation industry will create wealth and expand economy growth to any countries, but it will be accompanied by changed in the skills that workers need to learn. One of main ways that technology increases productivity is by decreasing the number of labor hours needed to create a unit of output. It implies (AI) technology will influence low educated and low skillful labor number to be decreased (reduction employment number).

In contrast, technological change tended to work in a different direction throughout the nowadays. The advance of computer and the internet raised the relative productivity of higher skilled workers. So, routine-intensive occupations that focused on predictable tasks disappearance, such as switch board, operators, filming checkers, travel agents and assembling line workers etc. were particularly replaced by new technologies.

However, today, it may be challenging to predict exactly which jobs will be most immediately affected by (AI) driven-automation. The reason is because (AI) is not a single technology, but rather a collection of technologies that are felt unevenly through the economy to influence job changing both negatively and positively. In positively view point, (AI) driven-automation will make many workers more productive and increase demand for certain skills. Consequently, new jobs are likely to be directly create in areas , such as the development and supervision of (AI) as well as indirectly created in a range of areas throughout the economy as higher incomes lead to expanded demand. Otherwise, in negatively view point, many traditional human needed (demand) skillful jobs will be threatened by automation are highly concentrated among lower-paid, lower-skilled and less -educated workers. It means automation will cause pressure on demand for this group, pressure and employment, if (AI) can replace the low skilled and less educated workers' jobs. Thus, (AI) will have negative influence to impact on the labor market.

(AI) capabilities will enable automation of some tasks that have long required human labor. Why can (AI) replace some simple human jobs? For example, advances in robotics are expanding machines' abilities to interact with and sharp the physical world. Combined , (AI) and robotics will give rise to smarter machines that can perform more sophisticated functions than ever before and brings more advantages that humans have exercised. This will permit automation of many tasks now performed by human workers and could change the shape of the labor market and human activity.

5.1 How (AI) influences labor market

Today, it may be challenging to predict exactly which jobs will be most immediately affected by (AI)-driven automation. Because (AI) is not a single technology, but rather a collection of technologies that are applied to specific tasks.

Some specific predictions are possible based on the current (AI) technology. For example, driving jobs and house cleaning jobs, bank counter service jobs, telephone enquiry service operators. Restaurant cooking jobs, simple accounting record service jobs etc. that require relatively less education to perform. Advancements in computer vision and related technologies have made the feasibility of fully appear more likely, potentially displacing some workers in driving-dominant professions. Seemingly similar robot, for which the operational tasks is less specific of navigating to a specific destination when following a set of given rules and preserving safety.

In the future, the effects of (AI) on the labor market in the decade ahead will continue the trend toward skill-biased change that computerization and communication innovations have driven in recent decades. Thus, some human driving occupation will be disappeared or replaced by (AI) automation driven. For example, bus drivers, light truck or delivery services drivers, heavy and tractor-trailer truck drivers, school drivers, tax drivers, travel bus drivers.

However, (AI) technology could enable some workers to focus time on other job responsibilities, boosting their productivity, and actually raised wage growth among those still holding the reshaped jobs. For example, salespeople, who currently spend a considerable amount of time driving could find themselves able to do other work when a car drives them from place to place, or inspectors and appraisers could fill out paperwork, when their car drives itself. This (AI) -driven technology should make these workers more productive, with (AI) -driven technology serving as a complement, not a substitute. New jobs will also likely be created, both in existing occupations cheaper transportation costs with lower prices and increase demand for products and all the related occupations, such as service and fulfillment, and in new occupations not currently foreseeable.

What kind of jobs will be created by (AI) technology? Predicting future job growth is extremely difficult, due to it depends on technologies or substitute for existing today as well as they may complement or substitute for existing human skills and jobs. However, (AI) will also lead to substantial indirect job creation to the degree it raises productivity and wages, it may also lead to higher consumption that would support additional jobs from high-end draft production to restaurant and retail. The future(AI) " augmented intelligence", the technology's role is as assisting and expanding the productivity of individuals rather than replacing human work. Thus, based on the biased-technical change framework, demand for labor will likely increase the most in the areas where humans complement (AI) automation technologies. For example, (AI) technology , such as IBM's Watson may improve early detection of some cancers or other illnesses, but a human healthcare professional is needed to work with patients to understand and translate patients' symptoms, inform patients of treatment options, and guide patients through treatment plans. Shipping companies may also partner workers who pick up and deliver products over the last feet with (AI) enabled autonomous vehicles that move workers efficiently from site to site. In such cases, (AI) augments what a human is able to do and allows individuals to either be move effective in their specially task or to operate on a larger scale. Thus, it seems (AI) technology will also create new jobs, raise productivities and workers' efficiencies.

5.2 Redefining management in
the workforce of artificial intelligence

In the future, due to artificial intelligence influences to some kind of human jobs nature. So, the kind of human jobs of management methods will also need to change to adapt the artificial intelligence technology input to their organizations. It will cause challenges for every executive and manager if who won't have effort to manage their teams how to apply artificial intelligence technology to work efficiently and easily. For example, division of labor will change among humans and machines will increase. Thus, companies will have to adapt their training performance and talent strategies how to emphasize on work that how to make human judgment and skills and experimentation. Thus, (IA)'s greatest impact will be on administrative coordination and control tasks, such as scheduling , resource allocation.

In fact, mangers will encounter this challenges: How to apply human experience and expertise to judge critical business decisions and practices when the information available is insufficient to suggest a successful course of action? Due to this kind of work will require new skills and mindsets. I shall indicate these change management methods to adapt (AI) technology. Such as: administration and routine tasks, scheduling , allocation of resources and reporting will fall within the intelligence machines, responsibilities that have long been reserved for humans. For example, a typical store manager or a lead nurse at a nursing home most constantly arrange shift schedules, accounting for staff members‘ absences owing to illness, vacation time or sudden departures.

Thus, the managers need to learn how to arrange new division of labor within the organizations after (AI) technology had been implemented to the organization. Artificial intelligence is currently influencing into once considered exclusive to humans: assessing and acting on human emotions and personality traits. The influences to managers need to change their strategies to adapt (AI) technology implements include such as below:

Firstly, managers need to spend the bulk of their time on coordination and control tasks from intelligent system implements. Their time spending on these major three aspects from impact of intelligent system: coordinate and control, solve problems and collaborate and people and community , strategy and innovation three aspects. Thus (AI) will influence managers need to change their judgment method to teach whose teams how to adapt the (AI) system operations in any organizations.

Secondly, (AI) will influence top, middle and low level management needs to change to adapt the (AI) technology operations to any owned (AI) technology organizations in the future. Intelligent machines must be trained in context. Just like humans , on-the-job training is a requirement for such machines because they typically arrive with only very general capabilities. To get the most from (AI), managers at all levels must participate in the instructional experience and in the learning process and provides managers' familiarity with such systems on these aspects, e.g. How the system works and generate advice, how the system has a proven track record , how the system provides convincing explanations , how the system can make simple rule- based decisions.

Thirdly, managers need to learn how to make judgment more accurate (AI) systems assistance. Although (AI) will invariably take on more routine work and even augment human decision-making, it won't judgment work, the application of human experience and expertise to critical business decisions when the information available is insufficient to suggest a successful course of action or reliable enough to suggest an obvious course of action. For a sense of the nature of judgment work, consider big data marketing and sales analytics. Such analytics often provide insights that can inform promotional campaigns, including predicting which promotions will generate desired sales brand further into the future, marketing executives need use judgment, combining analytics with their own and others' insight and experience.

The application of experience and expertise to critical business decisions and practice represents the real value of human judgment. But, when artificial intelligent machines are implemented to any organizations to assist the low, middle and top level management to make any business judgment. These forms of judgment work that managers can gather data interpretation, idea development more absolute from (AI) machine assistance. Thus, why these level management executives need to learn how to apply (AI) machines to help them to make any business judgment more accurate.

5.3 How (AI) influences organizational change

Consequently creative and social intelligence will be in even greater demand as (AI) makes in management and the workforce. This development will represent a long term trend in labor markets , one characterized by intensifying demand and reward for social skills with a growing desire for creative capabilities, managers will seek to fashion of ideas and hypotheses from inside and outside of the enterprise to shape solutions to their most pressing business problems. Thus, (AI) will influence overall organizational team members who have chance to participate any decision to make more accurate business judgment.

Many managers mistakenly view judgment work as only an individual discipline, failing to appreciate that it can also involve decide interpersonal and organizational practices. In more complex settings, judgment is typically a collective outcome of individuals' and teams' diverse perspectives, insights and experiences. And often , the resulting choices are better informed than decisions that an individual would have arrived at on his or her own.

Thus, when any organizations apply (AI) technology to assist managers to gather data and ideas to make any judgment. In these cases, organizations can create the conditions for effective collective judgment by establishing structures , such as " shadow advisory boards" that prompt managers and employees to source and synthesize multiple perspectives. Thus, a traditional organization (firm) might freshen its thinking is t put together a shadow advisory board, comprised of young, digital people who can apply (AI) machine assistance to make judgment work more accurate whether related to people development, problem-solving or strategizing and innovating for considerable degrees of creative and social intelligence.

Thus, on the one hand, (AI) technology machine augmentation and automation can give these advantages to human (organization managers) , e.g. developing people and community, solving problems and collaborating, coordinating and controlling work, shaping strategy and leading innovation. Besides, on the other hand, the next generation managers need have these individual attitude to treat intelligent machines to be as colleagues.

When, judgment is a human skill, intelligent machines can accelerate human learning that supports it, assisting in data -driven simulations, scenarios and search and discovery activities. Focuses on judgment work, some decisions require insight beyond what data can tell them. This is the sweet sport for human judgment, the application of experience and expertise to critical business decisions and practices. Thus, managers will also need to find ways to learn how to use digital (AI) technologies to tap into the knowledge and judgment of partners, customer external stakeholders and role models in other industries after the (AI) machine had been implemented to the organization.

5.4 Future works change:
Automation, employment
and productivity

Human future " micro to macro" industry trends will be affected business strategy and public policy by (AI) technology. In the future (AI) technology will influence those six themes: productivity and growth, natural resources, labor markets, the evolution of global financial markets, the economic impact of technology and innovation and urbanization. However, (AI) technology will bring economic benefits of tackling gender inequality, a new global competition, Chinese innovation and digital globalization.

Nowadays, advances in robotics artificial intelligence, and machine learning are in a new age of automation, as machines match or outperform human performance in a development to any countries. For example, automation of activities can enable businesses to improve performance by reducing errors and improving quality and speed, and in some cases achieving outcomes that go beyond human capabilities. For example, some research indicated automation could raise productivity growth globally by 0.8 to 1.4 % annually; more than 2,000 work activities across 800 occupations. When less than 5% of all occupations can be automated using demonstrated technologies about 60% of all occupations have at least 30% of constituent activities that could be automated. Many occupations will change that will be automated away: Activities most susceptible to automation involve physical activities, in highly structured and predictable environments, as well as the collection and processing of data. They are most prevalent in manufacturing , accommodation and food service and retail trade and include some middle-skill jobs. For example, such as natural language processing is a key factor. Beyond technical feasibility, the cost of technology competition with labor including skills and supply and demand dynamics, performance benefits including and beyond labor cost savings, and social and regulatory acceptance will be affected by (AI) automation technology. Thus, (AI) automation will impact to influence global employment in those aspects as below:

Firstly, assuming that people are displaced by automation will find other employment. The anticipated shift in the activities in the labor force is of a similar order as the long-term shift away from agriculture and decreases in manufacturing share of employment. Both of manufacturing and agriculture industries which would be accompanied by the creation of new types of work not foreseen at the time.

Secondly, for business, the performance benefits of automation are relatively clear. Thus, the businessmen have opportunities for their micro economies to benefits from the productivity growth potential and macro economies to benefit to encourage continued progress and innovation , investment and market incentives. At the same time, employers must innovate policies to help workers and institutions adapt to the impact on employment.

This will likely include rethinking education and training, income support and safety nets , as well as support for those dislocated, when employees need to leave themselves homes to move to other cities to learn new (AI) automation works. Thus, individuals in the workplace will need to engage move comprehensively with machines as part of their everyday activities, and acquire new skills that will be in demand in the new automation age. Consequently , the scale of shifts in the labor force over many decades that automation technologies can be a similar order to the long -term technology -enables shifts in the developed countries' workforces away from agriculture in the 21 th century. Those shifts did not result in long-term mass unemployment because they were accompanied by the creation of new types of work not foreseen at the time. However, human will still be needed in the workforce when the total productivity gains are caused by (AI) technology.

5.5 What occupations will be influenced by (AI) technology.

In the future, scientists predict that these occupations will be influenced by (AI) technology mostly. They include : retail salespeople, food and beverage service workers, language or translation teachers, health practitioners. Since these work activities have a more relevant occupations are made up of a range of activities with different potential for (AI) automation . For example, a retail salesperson will spend more time interacting with customers, stocking shelves , or ringing up sales. Each of these activities is distinct and requires different capabilities to perform successfully.

Thus, these job activities have similar simple control characteristics. Simple activities include greet customers, answer questions about products and services, clean and maintain work areas, demonstrate product feature process sales and transactions. All these activities can have similar simple activities in order to (AI) machines can be learn how to do these activities from (AI) technology . For example, the capability perception includes sensory perception, cognitive capabilities, such as retrieving automation, recognizing known patterns(supervised learning), logical reasoning problem solving.

Thus, (AI) machine is such human, which has feeling and emotion, such as social and emotional sensing, judgement reasoning methods, natural language understanding and physical capabilities, such as mobility , navigation, gross motor skill, fine motor skills. It seems that the future, (AI) human invents machines which will have these human characteristics to do human similar behavioral job duties more easily and efficiently. It

implies these above human occupations will be replaced by (AI) human invention machines in the future. Due to (AI) creation, it is possible to cause unemployment number of these above workers will increase because (AI) machines can do their similar job behavioral activities.
Consequently, employers won't need to employ many of these skillful labor. Otherwise, they can buy less number (AI) machines to attempt to do whose job activities more easily and efficiently. So, it seems (AI) machines will have more high work performance to replace these occupation workers' work performance. Finally, these occupation worker unemployment number will only increase when the (AI) machines had been invented to achieve to do their work behavioral activities absolutely success in the future.

5.6 Whether (A) technology machine labor will replace human worker more or assist human worker more

There is no single agreed definition of a robot how outcome of a task that is completed without human intervention. When some definitions require the task to be completed by a physical machine moves and respond to its environment, other definitions use the term robot in connection with tasks completed by software , without physical embodiment.
However, to answer the question : Whether (AI) technology machine labor will replace human worker more or assist human worker more. I shall indicate some examples to let readers to judge whether (AI) technology can create new jobs or reduce old jobs.
Firstly, I shall explain what (AI) function is. (AI) is a service robot that performs useful tasks for humans or equipment excluding industrial automation application . Thus, the classification of a robot into industrial robot or service robot is done according to its intended application. It is also a personal service robot or a service robot for personal used for a non commercial task, usually by lay persons . Examples are domestic servant robot, and pet exercising robot. It is also a professional service robot or a service robot for professional used for a commercial task, usually operated by a properly trained operator. Examples, are cleaning robot for public places, delivery robot in offices or hospitals, fire-fighting robot, rehabilitation robot and surgery robot in hospitals. Thus, these functions will be future (AI) application to our daily life necessaries or business necessaries.

However, some authors agree (AI) will bring negative outcomes of automation, due to raise competiveness, reduce human job nature. Otherwise, other authors argue (AI) will bring positive outcomes of automation, due to raise productivities, job creation, assist humans work.

On the positive outcome hand, robots can increase productivity . This is particularly important for small-to medium sized businesses both are in developed and developing countries economies. It also enables large companies to increase their competitiveness through faster product development and delivery. Increased use of robot is also enabling companies in high cost countries to re shore, or bring back to their domestic base parts of the supply chain that will have previously outsourced to sources of cheaper labor. Currently , the greater threat to employment is not a automation, but an inability to remain competitive. Automation has led overall to an increase in labor demand and positive impact on wages. The reason is that the middle-income/middle-skilled jobs have reduced as a proportion of overall contribution to employment and earnings leading to fears of increasing income inequality, the skills range within the middle income bracket is large. Thus, robots are driving an increase in demand for workers at the higher -skilled and with a positive impact on wages. This issue is how to enable middle-income earners in the lower-income range to unskilled or retain. Finally, the (AI) positive impact supporter who argue the future will be robots and humans can work together.

However, on the negative outcome hand, robots can substitute labor activities, but don't replace jobs. They believe that less than 10% of jobs are fully automatable. Increasingly , robots are used to complement and augment labor activities, the net impact on jobs and the quality of work is positive. Automation can provide the opportunity for humans to focus on higher-skilled, higher-quality and higher-paid tasks. Robots can improve productivity when they are applied to tasks that which perform more efficiently and to a higher and more consistent level of quality than humans. For example, increased productivity is enabling some firms, such as Whirlpool, Caterpillar and Ford Motors company in the US restructure their supply chains, bringing back parts of the manufacturing process to the country of origin. Thus, productivity gains due to robotics and automation are important not just at the company level, but also for build industry and nation competitiveness.

I suppose that productivity can be raised. What are the impacts of robots on employment? Firstly, the main focus of development has been on personal entertainment, which does not drive worker productivity (manufacturing production). When the internet (information and communication technology (ICT)) innovation. This is borne and by findings that manufacturing productivity, which has been driven by innovations in automation rather than consumer technologies, has government strongly than productivity in the services sectors of the economy in most nature economies. It seems (AI) automation will create many jobs in internet communication entertainment game industry. For example, many young people like to use internet to play any electronic games from computer or mobile at home or outside home conveniently. Thus, (AI) automation will increase demand to be invented to any new entertainment game from internet channel. It will need to employ many (AI) entertainment game inventors to create many automation entertainment games. Thus, (AI) automation in internet entertainment game industry will need human (AI) entertainment game inventors to invent the knowledge-based capital of (AI) automation entertainment games. The (AI) entertainment game inventors will need own research and development skills, form specific skills, organizational know-how skills, databased knowledge, design and various forms of intellectual property to do these (AI) automation entertainment game invention occupations in the future.

International Federation Of Robotics(2016) indicated that China will be as a major robotics manufacturer and user of robots, benefiting from jobs created by robot manufacturing and productivity gains from robot use. Chins had sold of robots to any one single market every year since 2017 year. The Chinese government has included a focus on robotics in its 10 year strategy. In order to achieve its target of a robot density of 150 units per 10, 000 workers by 2020 year. Thus, Chinese companies will have to install around 650,000 new industrial robots between 2016 to 2020 year, 2.5 times more than installed globally in 2015 year.

Hence, China (AI) manufacturing industry will need to employ many workers . It implies (AI) manufacturing industry will create many new occupations in China. Also, ministry of economy, trade and industry (2015) also showed that Japan currently has the largest stock of industrial robots in operations, primarily in the automation industry. Driven by a rapidly aging population and low productivity rates, the Japanese government has sights on a 20-fold increase in the use of robots in the non-manufacturing sector and a three-fold growth rate of labor productivity in the service sector both by 2020 year. Thus, it also implies Japan will need many robots to be provide to service industry. Due to robots will provide to serve any businessmen's clients. Thus, it is possible that the service workers won't be dismissed as well as it is depended on the serving job nature to decide whether Japan's service workers can still serve to their employer when the service (AI) robots are applied to whose employers.

Consequently, it seems that (AI) can create employment, Ministry of economy, trade and industry (2015) showed that such as China will develop the major (AI) automation manufacturing industry. The (AI) employers will need to employ many workers to manufacture any these different kinds of (AI) robots to satisfy China or overseas individual or business buyers needs. But, (AI) can also cause unemployment to the low skillful service workers. Such as if Japan some service businesses choose to buy any (AI) service robots to replace their service staffs to serve their clients. It is possible that the service staffs will be dismissed, due to (AI) robots can do such as their same service job duties to achieve better service performance. Thus, today, it is increasingly common for people to use robots in various situations at home and in retail stores, hotels and hospitals these service industries. Robots are classified into server types based on their functionality (service and utility robots or those designed to communicate with humans) and appearance (humanoid robots or mechanical robots). The type of robot, to which each country allocated particular importance in the advance of robotics, reflects the sense of values and preferences of its population. Thus, if the country has high population needs to use robots, then they will influence either more new jobs creation or more old job loss in the country's (AI) manufacturing or (AI) service industries both. For example, Japan respondents often associate the term " robot " with humanoid robots that can communicate with human and they have a high level of familiarity with robot. The US has the highest level of robot utilization at home and in retail stores with its people being the most enthusiastic about the future use of robots. Germany shows a strong tendency to consider robots for industrial purposes and its people feel strong effort to the presence of robots in their households.

In conclusion, to judge whether how (AI) will influence the country's employment to be better or worse. It will depend on the country home buyers (users) or business buyers (users) how to use (AI) for their daily needs. If the country , such as US retail stores need to use (AI) , it will have possible to reduce some or many retail service workers. Even, if the country , such as Japan has many home users need to use (AI) , it will not influence the employment market. Otherwise, it will raise (AI) salespeople numbers. Even, if the country, such as Germany and China will have many (AI) manufacturers, then it will create many (AI) manufacturing occupations for these (AI) manufactory workers.

Consequently, (AI) robots manufacturing and service needs will have positive or negative impact to any country's employment. It will depend on the (AI) service provision and service workers' job nature as well as the manufacturing workers of (AI) knowledge level to decide their employment chance in their country's employment market.

CHAPTER IV

(AI) -driven automation industry development

Nowadays, artificial intelligence (AI) is widely knowledge to be one kind of the dramatic technology. However, it is expected to continue, to have a disruptive impact on human's private and public life, so defense and security will be no exception. But how exactly will these be affected ? How will (AI) defense and security is incremental in nature?

To research why artificial intelligence (AI) has possible to be used to cause autonomous weapons by human. We need to understand these three aspects of relationship. They include cybersecurity and artificial intelligence and machine learning and autonomous weapon systems relationship between of them.

Firstly, we need to know what is the mean of artificial intelligence and cyber defense/offense? It means defense of critical networks: real time, pattern finding, anomaly seeking, it must utilize machine (AI) learning algorithms to efficiently, and instantaneously respond to potential network threats as well as it means human on or out of the loop. On the loop : it means anomaly detection: human notified, IT analysis, response. Out of the loop: it means anomaly detection: (AI) decides best method of response: quarantine, honey pot monitoring, hack-back. Thus, it is possible that (AI) can be used , such as autonomous cyber weapon.

What is artificial intelligence and autonomous weapons? Autonomous weapons mean one kind of weapon that can be selected and engaged a target, without intervention by a human operator. Are these machines artificially intelligent? I believe the answer is not, because present weapons systems are not capable of human level reasoning. But, (AI) algorithms are presently employed to process sensor data, monitor system health, take and respond to vocal commands manage data, navigate. This, future autonomous weapons systems will require stronger (AI) to be secure and operationally and cost effective. Moreover, self-aware autonomous cyber systems are crucial.

What is cybersecurity mean? It means the ability to control access to networked systems and the information they contain. It is acted to prevent , detect, recover, react. It is application objects concern people, process, technology and it's application goals are confidentiality, integrity and popular availability. Thus, what is cyber weapon mean? Walware means viruses, Trojans, zero-days, worms ransomware, spyware etc. Does it require a particular objective? E.g. military paramilitary or intelligence. Does it require physical harm? E.g. functional harm or interruption? Mental harm? Is (AI) a technological weapon that it is an object or tool? What about when it is an weapon agent?

In simplicity, (AI) can be one of scientific weapons platform. When one day, it is invented to be applied to control war planes to fly to any countries to attack enemies or it is invented to be seemed to human to replace soldiers to bring guns or any weapons go to other countries to attack. So, it is possible that future any war defense planes, (AI) technological automatic control weapon can be replaced of human soldiers or war plane pilots to control any war defense planes to go to different enemy countries to attack them easily. It is very horror matter to threaten global human's ourselves life in the future , if (AI) automatic control war defense planes or (AI) automatic control machine soldiers were invented successfully.

Hence , when (AI) can be applied to weapons platforms, it structures that launch weapons, i.e. jets, ships, vehicles. (AI) platform and weapon and software architecture components are be done one (AI) technological weapons systems. Thus, human will encounter any (AI) benefits or risks (threats) causes in the same time as soon as possible. If we can predict when (AI) weapon system will be manufactured or invented successfully. Then, we can reduce (AI) weapon systems risks , if we can threaten any (AI) scientists continue to invent any undiscovered (AI) weapons in any time to avoid the future first time (AI) weapon war occurrence in possible.

The (AI) weapon system risk means autonomy: the ability to problem solve technological war , when (AI) weapon system is manufactured successfully, the power to act, how to damage the (AI) weapon system. The power to chance to stop (AI) weapon system manufacturing processes, ability to create a new goals, how to change the (AI) weapon system inventors' or scientists' minds to avoid to apply (AI) tools to achieve attack goals to change to another positive goal. Due to human can't know a prior what an autonomous (AI) weapon system will do.

Although, human is known what (AI) is , but human is also known when (AI) scientists whose emergent behaviors will do to change to do any negative behaviors from positive behaviors. Whatever (AI) weapon system design we use, there will be cybersecurity, problems arising from computation design/complexity. Due to any one (AI) scientist can manipulate the system to act against itself, or who can utilize traditional " cyber weapons" against the (AI) weapon system, or who can manipulate the system to lie to humans, but also due to complexity, there is no way to know if it is lying or not or bounded rationality : satisficing.

Finally, the most serious (AI) technological invention risks are human is unknown these aspects of (AI) absolutely: They are not simple automatic systems, learning reasoning, communication of " self-aware" systems. Thus, human will face (AI) technological invention risks or threats. We need to find any methods to avoid (AI) weapon system is manufactured successfully to avoid (AI) technological war can occur in future anyone day. Consequently, why (AI) scientists do not choose to invent (AI) machine men own human reading, writing, speaking, judgement, analyizing abilities to develop human's future education industry, but they choose to invent (AI) machine men own human weapon to attack enemy ability.

Hence, (AI) scientists have moral responsibilities to avoid to invent (AI) machine men to own human's attack abilities. I shall indicate future what aspects of (AI) machine men can be applied to different education industry aspects as below:

8.1 Online technology and online book technology influences artificial intelligence mind development

Nowadays, online technological invention bring online book technological development. Also, artificial intelligent technological machine men had been invented to link internet to do any jobs, e.g. children can find any data from artificial intelligent machine men when the artificial intelligent machine man had been installed internet and computer function, then children can find any online books to read from the artificial intelligent machine man. Such as Japan artificial intellgent machine men had installed computer and internet function, the Japan family children can find any online books to read from the artificial intelligent machine man at Japan any families' homes conveniently. Hence, it implies that future one day, artificial intelligent machine has possible to be invented to own human's reading and/or writing abilities.

For example,online book publishing is one kind of popular internet technology. For example, Amazon publish is as a business model with many potential advantages, relative to a physical operation. It held out the potential of lower book inventing and distribution costs and reduced overhead. Consumers could find the books, they were looking for more easily and a variety book topic choices could be offered for sale. It can accept and fulfill orders from almost any domestic location with equal ease. And most purchasers made on its site would be exempt from sales tax. One Amazon strategy hand, it would have to make its returns and redress processes transparent and reliable, and offer other ways for clients to learn, as much about the book possible before buying. Future online book market development trend, such as Amazon, Barnes & Noble etc. online book shops.

Hence, online book store technology can be applied to artificial intelligent technology. Such as artificial intelligent machine men can apply computer technology to learn the abilities of reading and/or writing any books either on paper or on computer. Hence, it is possible that artificial intelligent machine men will have similar human's writing and/or reading books ability when they own human's mind ability. However, it bring this questions: Can artificial intelligent machine men own human's mind abilities? If they own human's mind abilities, is it mean that they can write and/or read any books? Can artificial intelligent machine men own human's mind abilities to create to write any books? Can artificial intelligent machine men own human's mind abilities to read and make any judgements or decisions more accurate than human's judgements or decisions? To answer these questions? I shall indicate that online book reading and writing technology can be applied to artificial intelligent machine men reading and writing technology. Because they are similiar computer mind technological development. So, I believe that future artificial intelligence machine men can be invented to own similar human's reading and writing's mind abilities in future one day.

I believe artificial intelligence and online technological reading abilities are very similiar. Nowadays, computer can be invented to attempt to read and write any books by human. Why can not artificial intelligent machine men replace computer to read and write any books? Artificial intelligent machine men can replace human to attempt to write or/and read books, due to artificial intelligent machine men had invented to own human mind to do some jobs and their mind had been invented to be similiar to human behavioral abilities to do these behaviors, e.g. cooking, driving, playing games, singing songs, speaking, listening, frighting etc. different human's abilities. So, it seems that artificial intelligent will be possible to be invented to own human's mind abilities to do any writing or reading behaviors or functions.

8.2 Prediction of artificial intelligence reading and writing abilities

development

What is future trend of artificial intelligence reading and writing abilities development? To answer this question, we need to know what benefits of artificial intelligent machine men can attribute to human's needs when they can own any human's mind to read or/and write any books.

I shall indicate e-books reading and writing example, if artificial intelligent machine men can be invented to own human's mind to write and/or read e-books on computer. Then, it brings this question: Can artificial intelligent machine men assist human to learn to do judgement to solve any challenges?

I believe that when artificial intelligent machine men can be invented to own human mind to write or/and read any books, then they will own human's mind ability to make judgement to solve any challenges more accurately, even their decisions can be more accurate to compare to human's decisions. So, artificial intelligent machine mens' writing and reading ability is the main factor to cause their mind to do any judgement in order to make any decisions more accurately. Consequently, in future one day, artificial intelligent machine mens‘ writing and reading ability will be invented to similar human's reading and writing abilities as well as their minds can also be invented to similar human's minds as well as their judgement abilities can be invented to similar to human's judgement abilities to make any decisions more accurate.

8.3 The influences when AI is invented to own human's mind and judgement abilities

Finally, I shall discuss what are the influences when AI is invented to own human's mind and judgement abilities in our future job market. The achievement of artificial intelligent (AI) machine men achievement requirement of owning human's mind and judgement abilities which requires extensive manual labor, and by augmenting the calling process with machine learning, the process where speed and accuracy are needed to close to human's mind and judgement abilities. Expert human race callers now have better information at artificial intelligent machine men at their fingertips faster.

Hence, if the above those requirements are achieved to satisfy artificial intelligent machine men ind and judgement abilities demand to close or exceed humans' mind and judgement abilities. Then, I believe that future human's some simple jobs must be replaced by (AI) machine men. Even, human's some professonal jobs, e.g. lawyer, accountant, administator, typing etc. professional skillful jobs, which will be either replaced or will be assisted by (AI) machine men. For example, (AI) machine men learn how to type english or other language words to do typing job ; they can learn how to apply accounting knowledge to record any firm's income and expenditure record of accounting job; they can also learn how to assist architects to design any architectural building drawing plans to do architect jobs; they can learn how to analyze any court evidences to judge any criminal or civil cases and assist lawyers to give legal advices to achieve more reasonable judgement for any legal cases; they can also learn how to assist firm's managers or administrators to manage any organization teams efficiently.

Consequently, when (AI) machine men can be invented to achieve to exceed human's mind and judgement abilities level. Then, I believe that they can do instead of human' simple jobs, which can do even human's more difficult and more judgement requirement of professional skillful jobs. So, (AI) machine men must need to achieve to do any jobs, they are same, even exceed to human professionals' abilities. Then, it will cause a lot of human's jobs to be disappeared or some human's jobs will be replaced by owning judgement and mind abilities of (AI) machine men to do.

Hence, future many human's jobs will be replaced by technological labors. Employers choose to buy (AI) machine men to replace human labors. The reasons include (AI) machine men have none unhappy, angry emotin to influence their low efficiencies and low productivities. Their judgement and mind abilities can exceed human's abilities or do any jobs to compare better performance to human's abilities. Consequently, different occupation labors need to prepare to learn how to co-operate with (AI) machine men to let future employers feel (AI) machine men will be human's assistant to assist human to do jobs efficiently when human and (AI) machine men work together. It aims to avoid future employers feel (AI) machine men's judgement and mind abilities can exceed any low knowledgeable and skilful occupation labors, even high knowledge and skilful occupation labors. It means that (AI) machine men are only labors' assistant if (AI) machine mens' judgement and mind abilities are below under to human labors' judgement and mind abilities.

Consequently, to avoid (AI) machine men can replace human to do any simple or complex jobs to cause any future any occupation labors' competitiors. I recommend that it is right time labors ought prepare to learn different skills. So, every individual labor does not only concentrate on one kind of skill. Because supposing one kind of the occupation labor's job duties are replaced by (AI) machine men. If the employee had owned more than one kind of occupation skill. Then, I believe that who can avoid the unemployment threat more easier than the employee only owned one kind of occupation skill, when (AI) machine men had invented to own human's mind and judgement abilities in future one day. The most important, I believe that (AI) invention will be applied to be teach how to learn human's skills and mind ability. Such as education industy, teacher won't be replaced by (AI), otherwise, (AI) will be teacher's assistant to help them to do education data gather or teaching jobs. So, teachers won't be replaced by (AI), otherwise, teachers will depend on (AI) data gather or teaching job to give them opinions how to solve student's teaching challenges as well as teachers can concentrate on researching education jobs for schools' benefits if (AI) technology can be invented to on human's mind and judgement and reading and writing abilities in the future.

8.4 Artificial intelligence and the future of defense or teaching choice

Nowadays, artificial intelligence (AI) is widely knowledge to be one kind of the dramatic technology. However, it is expected to continue, to have a disruptive impact on human's private and public life, so defense and security will be no exception. But how exactly will these be affected ? How will (AI) defense and security is incremental in nature? If (AI) technological machine men are applied to teach students in education aspect, is it better to my next generation learning develpment more than they are applied to war attack aspect.

To research why artificial intelligence (AI) has possible to be used to cause autonomous weapons by human. We need to understand these three aspects of relationship. They include cybersecurity and artificial intelligence and machine learning and autonomous weapon systems relationship between of them. Basic on (AI) machine can be invented to learn any new knowledge, so if (AI) machine men are taught how to attack enemy, which will be such as human soldier function. But, if (AI) machine men are taught how to learn university knowledge to teach students. Then, they will be such as human lecturer function. So, when (AI) is invented to own human mind and judgement and learning abilities, then they will be either human's enemy or human's assistant, such as university lecturer's assistant.

Firstly, we need to know what is the mean of artificial intelligence and cyber defense/offense? It means defense of critical networks: real time, pattern finding, anomaly seeking, it must utilize machine (AI) learning algorithms to efficiently, and instantaneously respond to potential network threats as well as it means human on or out of the loop. On the loop : it means anomaly detection: human notified, IT analysis, response. Out of the loop: it means anomaly detection: (AI) decides best method of response: quarantine, honey pot monitoring, hack-back. Thus, it is possible that (AI) can be used , such as autonomous cyber weapon. If (AI) is applied to make the decision best method of response to learning aspect, such as univeristy different subject knowledge. Then, it will be one good technological educational tool to teach university students.

In simplicity, (AI) can be one of scientific weapons platform or one of university teaching tool. When one day, it is invented to be applied to control war planes to fly to any countries to attack enemies or it is invented to be seemed to human to replace soldiers to bring guns or any weapons go to other countries to attack. So, it is possible that future any war defense planes, (AI) technological automatic control weapon can be replaced of human soldiers or war plane pilots to control any war defense planes to go to different enemy countries to attack them easily. It is very horror matter to threaten global human's ourselves life in the future , if (AI) automatic control war defense planes or (AI) automatic control machine soldiers were invented successfully. Otherwise, when one day, (AI) machine lecturer is invented to be applied to learn university different subjects knowledge to replace lecturers to copy lecturer's every prepared lecturer course to speak to let students to listen when they are sitting in university halls as well as the (AI) machine lecturer can make analysis and judgement response to answer every student's enquire immedicately after it had speaking all courses to students to listen in lecturer hall every time. Then, it can let human lecturer does any education job duty, e.g. research education work. So, (AI) machine lecturer will be future human lecturer's assistant in future one day.

Finally, the most serious (AI) technological invention risks are human is unknown these aspects of (AI) absolutely: They are not simple automatic systems, learning reasoning, communication of " self-aware" systems. Thus, human will face (AI) technological invention risks or threats if human invent (AI) machine man to learn how to attack enemy. Otherwise, if human invent (AI) machine man to learn how to teach univerity student. I believe that my future university students can raise learn ability and writing ability and reading ability from (AI) machine lecturer teaching more than human lecturer teaching.

8.5
Online technology and online book technology influences artificial intelligence mind development

Nowadays, online technological invention bring online book technological development. Also, artificial intelligent technological machine men had been invented to link internet to do any jobs, e.g. children can find any data from artificial intelligent machine men when the artificial intelligent machine man had been installed internet and computer function, then children can find any online books to read from the artificial intelligent machine man. Such as Japan artificial intellgent machine men had installed computer and internet function, the Japan family children can find any online books to read from the artificial intelligent machine man at Japan any families' homes conveniently. Hence, it implies that future one day, artificial intelligent machine has possible to be invented to own human's reading and/or writing abilities.

For example,online book publishing is one kind of popular internet technology. For example, Amazon publish is as a business model with many potential advantages, relative to a physical operation. It held out the potential of lower book inventing and distribution costs and reduced overhead. Consumers could find the books, they were looking for more easily and a variety book topic choices could be offered for sale. It can accept and fulfill orders from almost any domestic location with equal ease. And most purchasers made on its site would be exempt from sales tax. One Amazon strategy hand, it would have to make its returns and redress processes transparent and reliable, and offer other ways for clients to learn, as much about the book possible before buying. Future online book market development trend, such as Amazon, Barnes & Noble etc. online book shops.

Hence, online book store technology can be applied to artificial intelligent technology. Such as artificial intelligent machine men can apply computer technology to learn the abilities of reading and/or writing any books either on paper or on computer. Hence, it is possible that artificial intelligent machine men will have similar human's writing and/or reading books ability when they own human's mind ability. However, it bring this questions: Can artificial intelligent machine men own human's mind abilities? If they own human's mind abilities, is it mean that they can write and/or read any books? Can artificial intelligent machine men own human's mind abilities to create to write any books? Can artificial intelligent machine men own human's mind abilities to read and make any judgements or decisions more accurate than human's judgements or decisions? To answer these questions? I shall indicate that online book reading and writing technology can be applied to artificial intelligent machine men reading and writing technology. Because they are similiar computer mind technological development. So, I believe that future artificial intelligence machine men can be invented to own similar human's reading and writing's mind abilities in future one day.

I believe artificial intelligence and online technological reading abilities are very similiar. Nowadays, computer can be invented to attempt to read and write any books by human. Why can not artificial intelligent machine men replace computer to read and write any books? Artificial intelligent machine men can replace human to attempt to write or/and read books, due to artificial intelligent machine men had invented to own human mind to do some jobs and their mind had been invented to be similiar to human behavioral abilities to do these behaviors, e.g. cooking, driving, playing games, singing songs, speaking, listening, frighting etc. different human's abilities. So, it seems that artificial intelligent will be possible to be invented to own human's mind abilities to do any writing or reading behaviors or functions.

8.6 Prediction of artificial intelligence reading and writing abilities

development

What is future trend of artificial intelligence reading and writing abilities development? To answer this question, we need to know what benefits of artificial intelligent machine men can attribute to human's needs when they can own any human's mind to read or/and write any books.

I shall indicate e-books reading and writing example, if artificial intelligent machine men can be invented to own human's mind to write and/or read e-books on computer. Then, it brings this question: Can artificial intelligent machine men assist human to learn to do judgement to solve any challenges?

I believe that when artificial intelligent machine men can be invented to own human mind to write or/and read any books, then they will own human's mind ability to make judgement to solve any challenges more accurately, even their decisions can be more accurate to compare to human's decisions. So, artificial intelligent machine mens' writing and reading ability is the main factor to cause their mind to do any judgement in order to make any decisions more accurately. Consequently, in future one day, artificial intelligent machine mens' writing and reading ability will be invented to similar human's reading and writing abilities as well as their minds can also be invented to similar human's minds as well as their judgement abilities can be invented to similar to human's judgement abilities to make any decisions more accurate.

8.7 The influences when AI is invented to own human's mind and judgement abilities

Finally, I shall discuss what are the influences when AI is invented to own human's mind and judgement abilities in our future job market. The achievement of artificial intelligent (AI) machine men achievement requirement of owning human's mind and judgement abilities which requires extensive manual labor, and by augmenting the calling process with machine learning, the process where speed and accuracy are needed to close to human's mind and judgement abilities. Expert human race callers now have better information at artificial intelligent machine men at their fingertips faster.

Hence, if the above 'those requirements are achieved to satisfy artificial intelligent machine men ind and judgement abilities demand to close or exceed humans' mind and judgement abilities. Then, I believe that future human's some simple jobs must be replaced by (AI) machine men. Even, human's some professonal jobs, e.g. lawyer, accountant, administator, typing etc. professional skillful jobs, which will be either replaced or will be assisted by (AI) machine men. For example, (AI) machine men learn how to type english or other language words to do typing job ; they can learn how to apply accounting knowledge to record any firm's income and expenditure record of accounting job; they can also learn how to assist architects to design any architectural building drawing plans to do architect jobs; they can learn how to analyze any court evidences to judge any criminal or civil cases and assist lawyers to give legal advices to achieve more reasonable judgement for any legal cases; they can also learn how to assist firm's managers or administrators to manage any organization teams efficiently.

Consequently, when (AI) machine men can be invented to achieve to exceed human's mind and judgement abilities level. Then, I believe that they can do instead of human' simple jobs, which can do even human's more difficult and more judgement requirement of professional skillful jobs. So, (AI) machine men must need to achieve to do any jobs, they are same, even exceed to human professionals' abilities. Then, it will cause a lot of human's jobs to be disappeared or some human's jobs will be replaced by owning judgement and mind abilities of (AI) machine men to do.

Hence, future many human's jobs will be replaced by technological labors. Employers choose to buy (AI) machine men to replace human labors. The reasons include (AI) machine men have none unhappy, angry emotin to influence their low efficiencies and low productivities. Their judgement and mind abilities can exceed human's abilities or do any jobs to compare better performance to human's abilities. Consequently, different occupation labors need to prepare to learn how to co-operate with (AI) machine men to let future employers feel (AI) machine men will be human's assistant to assist human to do jobs efficiently when human and (AI) machine men work together. It aims to avoid future employers feel (AI) machine men's judgement and mind abilities can exceed any low knowledgeable and skilful occupation labors, even high knowledge and skilful occupation labors. It means that (AI) machine men are only labors' assistant if (AI) machine mens' judgement and mind abilities are below under to human labors' judgement and mind abilities.

Consequently, to avoid (AI) machine men can replace human to do any simple or complex jobs to cause any future any occupation labors' competitiors. I recommend that it is right time labors ought prepare to learn different skills. So, every individual labor does not only concentrate on one kind of skill. Because supposing one kind of the occupation labor's job duties are replaced by (AI) machine men. If the employee had owned more than one kind of occupation skill. Then, I believe that who can avoid the unemployment threat more easier than the employee only owned one kind of occupation skill, when (AI) machine men had invented to own human's mind and judgement abilities in future one day.

8.8 Why does AI machine lecturer can raise education quality?

When (AI) machine men can own human reading and writing and judgement and analytical abilities, then they can replace university lecturers to teach students to raise students' learning abilities absolutely. Then, it bring this question: Why does I machine lecturer can raise education quality? Why do universities prefer to apply (AI) machine lecturer to teach teachers more than human lectuer in university lecturer hall learning environment? Will (AI) university lecturers replace human lecturers to teach students to learn at university lecturing halls popularly? Can (AI) university lecturers replace university human lecturers to teach students more easily and it can let students feel more easily to learn when they are listening what (AI) university lecturers are teaching to them every time university lecture.

In university today, nearly all students need to attend university lecturing hall to listen their lecturer's teaching in every time course. However, many students do not feel interesting to attend university halls to listen human lecturer's teaching. The reasons include, they are busy, so no time to attend lecturer's hall to listen lecturer's teaching; or they feel bore to listen their lecturer's teaching; they feel difficulty to learn; they have confidence to exam and do their assignments, so they feel that they do not need to go to lecturing halls to listen their human lecturer's teaching. However, if one day, (AI) machine lecturers are invented to teach university students to learn and solve their learning difficulties. Can it raise student individual learning interest, due to (AI) machine lecturers' education quality is better than human lecturers' education quality?

What will influence to university students if (AI) machine lecturer can invented to replace human lecture? The influences will include such as below:

First reason: the only way is going to be useful to university lecturers are if all (AI) machine lecturers are well-informed and fully supported to assist human lectuers to teach whose students to let them to listen whose teaching absolutely. So, human lecturers can concentrate on doing any education research and data gathering jobs to prepare for (AI) machine lecturers to help them to explain human lecturers' every time prepared course contents more efficiently. So, (AI) machine lectuers can help human lecturers to share whose teaching time in lecturing halls. Human lecturers' can spend whose hall lecturing time to do whose educational research or other educational gathering jobs absolutely.

The second reason, the human lecturer (Human capital) has ability and efficiency of concentrating on education data gatehering research jobs to prepare to write whose books. When (AI) machine lecturer replace the human lecturer to spend time to attend lecturing hall to teach students. Fo long term, the human lecturer can raise education productivity growth and education quality raising, due to who only concentrate on searching or gathering data to prepare to write whose books to raise their education level.

In macro and micro economic view, the well (AI) machine lecturer educated labor (human capital) is often replaced to human lecturer as one of the critical factors to influence rapid education productivities and educational quality growth to the Asia developing countries' any regions or cities. Because any of these Asia developing countries, such as China, Korea, Philippines etc. countries which need have well educated and knowledgeable lecturer labors to raise any universities' educational productivities and educational qualities growth. So (AI) assistant lecturer factors which ought have close relationship to cause the good or bad future student learning effectiveness and education or learning qualities raising in these any one of Asia developing countries.

The third reason, for the big population of student growth number example, China's student growth rate is larger than school growth rate. If China expect every students have enough chance to study in schools, but university human lectuer numbers are not enough to supply to universities to teach their students. I believe that (AI) machine lecturer is only one kind of teaching method to solve these big population countries' university lectuer number shortage challenge.

In conclusion, in long term, (AI) machine lecturers can solve university human lecturer shortage challenge as well as they can attract many students to attend lecturing halls and human lecturers can raise education quality when they can concentrate on searching or gathering data to prepare their education career, when (AI) machine lectuers replace them to spend time to attend univesity halls to teach students in every university lecturing time.

8.9

Future AI machine education market

I believe that when AI (artificial intelligent machine men) which can invented to own to similar to human mind, learning, language, analytical, judgement abilites. Then, which can be applied to any education market service industy. (AI) potential education market service industy includes such as below:

- (AI) university lecture assistant

Future (AI) machine men can assist univerity lectuers to attend university halls to attempt to teach university students for different subjects, e.g. english, math, economic, math, engineering, art, architect etc. different subjects. It depends on the human lectuter who prepares to spend time to teach the (AI) machine lecturer to remember whose teaching subject. For example, the economic lecturer spend one year time to teach the (AI) machine lecturer to learn all economic knowledge. Then, the (AI) machine lecturer can use its machine brain to remember all the human lecturer's economic concepts and prepared teaching economic contents within the one year. Hence, after one year the (AI) machine lecturer can remember all the human lecturer's economic concepts and economic theories and economic contents to prepare to attend university lecturing halls to teach all first year undergraduated first year economic students confidently. It means that the human lecturer's job duties will change to teach (AI) machine lecturer to learn whose economic knowledge to prepare to let the (AI) machine lecturer to replace whom to teach whose university students; so the human lectuer can spend more time to do other research job for whose university education development. Hence, the (AI) machine lecturer can share the human lecturer teaching job as well as the human lectuer can concentrate on spending time to do whose research jobs for whose university education development. This is one both win strategy to university and the lecturer if (AI) machine lecturer is invented to assist future university lecturer's teaching jobs

● (AI) secondary and primary teacher assistant

In the future (AI) technolgical development, instead of (AI) machine men can be applied to university education aspect. Future (AI) machine men can also be applied to secondary and primary teaching aspect. For example, primary and secondary schools do not need attend classroom to teach students. (AI) machine teachers can replace them to attempt to do teaching job. They only need to spend one year time to prepare to teach (AI) machine teacher to learn how to apply their teaching skill concern their subjects who need to teach to their students, e.g. english language writing and reading and spelling skill, sing song skill, drawing picture skill, calculation skill etc. different studying skill. Then, the (AI) primary or secondary machine teacher can apply the primary or sendary human teacher skills to attempt yo teach whose students. Hence, the primary and secondary human teacher whose duties will change to learn how to teach whose teaching skills to let the (AI) primary or seondary machine lecturer to remember how to apply human skills to teach whose students for different subjects, such as, english writing and reading and spelling language skills, singing songs language skills, math calculation skills etc. Hence, future primary or secondary school teachers who responsibilities will change to learn how to teach (AI) machine teacher teaching skills to prepare to replace them to teach their students in classroom.

● (AI) scientific research assistant

Futurc (AI) machine men can be applied to science research aspect, instead of school education job. For example, (AI) machine men can be any scientist's assistant, e.g. space scientist, earth or ocean scientist, human or animal behavioral psychological scientist, climate scientist, chemical scientist, drug scientist etc. How can (AI) machine men can be any kind of scientist to assist scientists to do research jobs ? I shall indiate such as below: For space science example, the (AI) machine space scientist can assist human space scientist to gather space data to assist space scientist to research any undiscovered material to cause our earth, even space. Hence, the space scientist only need to teach the (AI) machine scientist to learn how to help them to apply space technological tools to gather data and then enter all data to computer to record, even the (AI) machine scientist can store all space data discovered record to their machine brain every day. Hence, the human space scientist does not need to spend much time to do gathering data job. The (AI) machine space scientist can help whom to do these space data gathering job, then the human space scientist can concentrate on spendin time to do space research job in whose space science laboratory every day.

For earth science example, the (AI) machine earth scientist can help the earth scientist to go to anywhere to gather earth or ocean natural activity data in our earth every day. Then, the earth scientist only need sit in whose earth laboratory to wait the (AI) machine earth scientist to come to whose laboratory to give whose gathering every day earth or ocean natural activity data to do future research job. Hence, the earth scientist does not need to leave whose laboratory to do any data gathing jobs concern earth or ocean natural activities. The (AI) machine earth or ocean scientist had helped him/her to go to our earth or ocean anywhere to do any earth or ocean activities data gathering jobs every day. Hence, the earth or ocean scientist can concentrate on spending whose time to do any research jobs in laboratory. It means that the (AI) machine earch or ocean scientist had replaced whom to do all outdoor original gathering data jobs.

For these human or animal behavioral psychological scientist, climate scientist, chemical or drug scientist, scientist all examples, the (AI) machine human or animal behavioral psychological scientist can help them to do any data gathering job, e.g. the (AI) machine scientist can learn how to help human or animal behavioral psychological scientist to contact human or animal to observe their daily activities and record all their activities data to transfer all these daily activites data to let the human or animal behavioral psychological scientist to do psychological researching analysis only. The (AI) machine climate scientist can help the human climate scientist to arrive anywhere to observe climate changes and record climate changes daily. Then, the human climate scientist only need to wait the (AI) machine climate scientist's gathering climate change data record from whose machine brain to do climate changing predict research job in climate laboratory every day. The (AI) chemical or drug machine scientist can help the drug or chemical scientist to gather data of new drug or chemical from internet channel every day. So, the human chemical or drug scientist only need to do researching job after the (AI) machine scientist transfers all daily chemical or drug information to let them to know from internet channel. It means that the chemical or drug human scientist does not need to spend much time to gather drug or chemical new data development trend from internet. The (AI) machine chemical or drug scientist had helped them to do data gathering job every day.

Consequently, future (AI) machine men can do education and research aspects of jobs duties and their role are only human scientists or primary or secondary teachers or university lecturers whose assistants either to share scientist's data gathering job or share teachers or lecturers' teaching job.

CHAPTER V

Can non-manual driving public transport tools bring global economic growth

Can robots help non-manual driving vehicle development to grow global economic development ?

● Reasons we need to improve public bus transport tool service quality

The ways that we need to improve public transport, e.g. bus transport service, we try our best to ask these questions: During periods of stress on the bus, like weather conditions or maintenance failure that slows the bus service system? How to improve mass transit on bus service frequency, when looking at ways to improve public bus service transport , riders want frequency? Interestingly, speed is not as much of an issue, if they are waiting downtown in the rain, or on some suburban backstreet, riders want to know that a bus will arrive soon, preferably in less than 15 minutes. Therefore, the wait becomes part of the transportation cycle. Even, if the bus is lightning fast, in the mind of the rider, the trip begins right when they arrive at the bus station, and start waiting for the bus to pick them up.

`

`What does efficient bus ticketing system mean? It is big part of how to improve bus transportation efficiency is improving transit ticketing system, because ticketing systems have to be quick and practical to allow for prompt loading and unloading of passengers. So, inefficient ticketing systems also slow down bus frequency, as drivers need to wait for everyone to tap before they can drive away to the next stop.

How to let passengers feel comfortable? Riders want comfortable buses that can seat as many people as possible. Face-to-face seating is not appealing and being knee-to-knee in a confined space creates awkward moments between strangers. However, comfort also extends beyond the buses' seating arrangements. A smooth riding, quiet bus plays a significant role in reducing the overall stress of a public transit experience. Among the consistent feedback from riders of fuel cell electric buses is a surprised delight about how quiet the buses are when in motion.

On reduce greenhouse gases environment prote3ctoin aspect, exhaust spewing buses are on ongoing concern. One of the significant factors that commuters consider when deciding to take public transit is the environment impact of their alternative transport method. And although a diesel bus packed with 40 people may be less environmentally damaging than 40 separate diesel cars, it will still have negative impacts on both local air quality and the overall climate situation , when given the choice, we've found nearly all riders prefer " zero-emission buses" to conventional diesel buses nowadays.

IN fact, we are always thinking of ways to improve public transportation by dev4eloping new clean fuel technologies. Fuel cell electric buses resolve some of the above issues for both transit bus operators, bus performance is continually being proven and improved over millions of miles of operation in environments ranging from mountain villages to desert communities to busy cities. Hence, the first step to creating better public transit networks is becoming aware of the available options. Many communities are taking measures to improve public transport by implementing innovative sustainable transport solutions that have profound impacts on the live ability of their communities.

So, I shall recommend these ways to improve public transport methods to bus service as below:

Firstly, making interchanging easy for public transport has most efficient public transport service improvement aim at linking areas that are outside a city to the city center., doing this is beneficial in two ways. It helps people who should not at the city center , but needed to pass through because the outlying areas are not connected together to keep off and hence reduce congestion at the center. Also, connecting the outlying areas provide a backup for the public transport system in case of a problem which often happen.

Secondly, minimize the number of stops/ stations, stops and stations improve the efficiency of public transport , but there should be a balance between enabling accessibility with more steps or stations and reducing the costs of operation by increasing transit need of ensure trips are covered in time. Therefore, core should be taken to ensure that stops and stations are located on streets to balance accessibility by commuters on one hand and reduces operating cost on the other hand.

Thirdly, lessen traffic congestion by deploying a number measures. Reducing traffic congestion at city streets could be done, implementing a number of strategies, such as providing lanes dedicated specially for the use of public transport, deploying strict regulations , such as queue bypasses or queue jumps. Another means of reducing traffic congestion is by providing feeds and data from public transport systems, freely to commuters to educate and help them avoid areas of traffic congestion and finally, giving priority to public and trams operating efficiency, increasing the travel time of these engineering mechanism whereby a traffic signal turns green at the light of a public transport at an intersection. All of above these improvements may be future public transport bus passengers service improvement need, if any bus companies hope to increase their bus passengers number absolutely.

- What rail passengers really want rail innovation improvement

Public transport systems, such as rail provides benefits including less traffic congestion, less pollution, safe travels, lower expenditures , less effort and better predictability in comparison to road transport. In fact, bus and train riders experience the most negative emotions in comparison with other transport modes, such as private cars , walking and cycling. Hence, technology has the potential to bring about the changes, needed to increase efficiency of rail transport, e.g. cost-effective ways to improve the quality of public transport and increase ridership may involve comfort and convenience improvement, or technology has the potential to provide more up-to-date information and customized service to train passengers and therefore improve the rail journey experience . On the overall, passenger journey , e.g. the importance of automated traveller information systems, and electronic fare payment collection systems can bring rail passengers look for this information in different interfaces from localized displays installed on platforms to smartphone applications.

Moreover, technology can also improve fare collection and management which of made manually can be prone to error, and time consuming , unified cards, smartphones can make it easier for rail passengers to obtain ticket, with the potential to increase the user satisfaction with the rail system. Because rail passengers demand not only pre-trip information for planning their travels, but also information during journeys, such as punctuality, connections and platform allocation. One extensive review indicates that accurate communication, for example, giving effective way finding information, can optimize passengers' experience with public transport.

Also, technology can facilitate the process of finding free seats on trains, which is a current demand from rail passengers and the cause of stress during the boarding process. IN fact, many rail passengers have specific preferences regarding seats and would appreciate having control of where to sit. So, navigation and way finding information can be delivered directly to passengers to inform where they could stand aiming to board less busy carriages, for example, choosing to travel on a less crowded train, or spreading themselves out on the platform before boarding in respond to crowding information, e.g. smartphones are frequently used by passengers of public transport and can make waiting times seem shorter. Furthermore specific system features designed for train passengers have the potential to improve the journey experience of the travelling public.

What ferry passengers service improvement need

● How can ferry service be improved affordable, reliable, convenient, flexible and clean will get drivers out of their cars ad onto environmentally responsible to passenger ferries?

Ferry transportation provides an environmentally friendly commuting alternative to the congested roadways in many of countries , so ferry transport service needs to meet long term air quality goals, it is critical to move beyond traditional technologies to zero-and near zero emissions technology. Clearly putting a transit system in operation that demonstrates emission control technology and the development of zero-emissions, ferries will help achieve air quality goals to our societies, for example., new shipping rout4es are needed to increase in order to satisfy ferry passengers different rapid ferry journey short distance need, when they need to choose one kind of public transport service either bus or rail or ferry transport service among of them.

None ferry accident occurrence, ferry service needs to let passengers to feel it is the safest sea pubic transit, expanded recreational service is also needs, particularly on weekends when bridge , corridor traffic congestion is becoming an increasing problem. Ferry service needs have uniquely provided flexible, vital transportation supports in response to a natural or man-made disaster that shuts down bridges and roads, fuel –cell technology is needed , that will lead to zero-emissions ferries, e.g. on-board emissions monitoring is far less polluting than previously through, e.g. 149 passenger boats are designed to travel 25 knots or less , and 300-350 passenger vessels designed for speeds up to 30-35 knots.

This emissions standard will perform specifications and the cost of this technology is accounted for in the ferry company vessel capital budget ,e.g. vessel design capabilities to accommodate existing and new docking configurations . This maximizes fast ferry passenger loading, including bicycles, carriages and wheelchairs. Hence, future global ferry service needs have these positive influence to our societies: Need for flexibility, desire to help the environment, need for time saving, which includes the importance of reliability, sensitivity to personal travel experience, such as a need for personal space or quiet feeling ferry seat any time, insensitivity to transport cost, e.g. the ferry ticket price is cheaper than rail or bus fares sensitivity to stress.

However, ferry service is different unlike rail, bus because expanded ferry service can be launched quickly at low initial cost and with great flexibility. Unlike buses, ferries are not hindered by traffic congestion on roads and highways or in tunnels. So, ferry service can be safely expanded to bring new service to new places and add more service to existing routes more easily than bus and rail public transport both, e.g. expanded ferry transport service can operate safety and provide with a robust, flexible and effective emergency response capability if the region is hit with a natural or man-made event that disables roads, other transit, bridges , before any.

Hence, ferry companies need to decide to improve their ferry transport service, they need to answer these questions: Is the new shipping route a good transportation investment? Does the new shipping route have fatal environmental negative impact? Does it offer a transit option that can be initiated in a timely and cost-effective manner? Can it provide ferry transport service that is reliable, safe and fully accessible after the ferry recovery would be unreasonably high charge to ferry selection is decided to implement to increase?

Also, ferry safety is needed to consider because it can influence any ferry passenger choice, when the ferry is moving on the sea, when the passenger is sitting on the boat. The ferry safety issue may include: Ensuring that access to all ferry operational areas, including, machinery spaces, pilothouse and gear lockers, remain locked at all times and accessible only to authorized crew, posting night watch security guards at terminals, conducting diligent onboard inspection for unattended passenger bags, briefcases and packages after each run, before the next boat load is allowed to board, creating coded signals and response to report suspicious activity, requiring positive identification before allowing any contractors, vendors or others access to ferries, providing additional security training to crew, developing a security plan to account for potential threats, outlining preventive measures and detailing an action plan in the event of a threat or actual emergency.

Future Human Transport Need Change

How future our transport need change? What factors influence our future transport need change? In general, these factors may influence our transportation need change. They may include fuel cost, the labor market for commercial drivers, demand for frieight , customer loyalty , vehicle capacity, government regulation, geographical events, the public transport tool reputation to passegners as a merchant. However, the factors that influence the development of transport system in an area? They may include as below:

Environment at the local scale existing hydrographical and geomorphological characteristics are string, factors in transport development, particularly in terms of the technical challenges (bridge, gradients,) they present to construct, other factors may include historical, technological, political and economic factors. All of these factors may influence our future transport system how develops. For raiway development influential factors, they may include: Geograohical factors, e.g. the North Indian plain with its level land, high density of population and rich agriculture presents the most favourable conditions for the development of railways in India. However, the presence of large number of rivers makes it necessary to construct bridges which involve heavy expenditure to Indian Government publich transport expenditure.

How transport has changed from past to present?

There has been a remarkable development in modern transportation. The stream engine and then the stream trains have emerged and spread at this time and in abundance until the discovery of natural gas and oil was an evolution of transportation. Thus, the sedams and vehicles began to run in oil, until present battery changes energy vehicle need, even future non-manual driving artificial intelligent driving vehicle need. These new transport technology may influence our future public transportation from gas energy to battery changed energy, even non-manual driving vehicles need to our daily transport need.

So, our future purpose of public transport need is the unique purpose to oversome space, which is shaped by a variety of human and physical constraints, such as distance, time. These both is our future main public transport need main purpose factors, short distance and reducing journey time, they influence that why we need to choose to catch any kinds of public transportation tool to replace purchase private cars to drive transport tool choice. So, future any kinds of public transport tools, they need to consider above both main factors , how to attract passengers to choose to catch themselves public transport tools choice in this competitive public transport tools market.

On the other hand, the economic importance of transportation development can be defined as improving the welfare of a society, through appropriate social, political and economic conditions , such as US Government spent too much money to assist MTR (MAss transport railway firm) to develop underground thrain transport. Its aim to let many passegner can reduce journey time and reduce distance between destinations, it also hopes US citizen passengers can pay cheap transport fare to buy ticket to catch underground transport train for many families their transport expenditure in social transport welfare view.

However, US Government neds to solve those challenges, before it implements to develop rapid underground railway , e.g. lack of knowledge of geographical fwatures, lack of manpower necessary to operate the rapid underground railway construction work, lack of construction materials within the US itself. For Brazil rail network transportation development example, the factors influence the use of rail network for transportion is highly restricted in Brazil. Thus, the development of roadways and waterways is the main modes of transportation that caould be used in Brazil given its topography and drainage benefit to society . So, brazil can develop rail network for transportation development in success.

So, transportation system is important in the development of any nation, because transportation plays important role in rapid economic growth of a nation. Thrapsortation increases the quality and variety of consumer goods, thereby stimulating the demand and development of trade and economy of the nation. Moreover, transport provides various employment opportunities and boosts up the economy of the country.

Also, any transport tools need to improve themselves transport service in order to attract passengers to choose their public transport service more easily. They may attempt to sign up for an autonomous vehicle pilot program, free phone enquiey concerns whether the passegner can catch which bus bumber to go to the destination, hou much bus fare, how long journey time, when the bus will arrive teh bus stops or leave the bus stop etc. bus service questions, before any one passenger prepares to choose to catch bus (free bus go phone call enquiry), free download a public transport tool transit app. even water taxi tranport tool innovation can replace ferry public transport tool, it can let passengers have more fun an enjoyable catching feeling. So, water taxi tranport tool is one kind of future new transport tool change to replace ferry , it can influence ferry passengers to choose water taxi public transport tool to replace ferry. Although, its fare may be more expsnse to compare ferry, but it can reduce jounrey time and distance between both water stations, when ferry can not arrive the other destinations, but water taxi can arrive any one water station destination. It can bring convenient to future any one ferry passengers. So, water taxi may be developed to some countries, e.g. New Zealand , Auckland city, US , Washington and New York cities they had developed water taxi public transport tools to let ferry passengers have one kind new water public transport choice.

However, instead of new transport innovation improvement to water transport service public transport with input from the public on bus transport service aspect, bus frequency improvement, it means when booking at ways to improve, bus frequency from long times to less times, efficient bus ticketing system, a big part of how to improve tranportation efficiency is improving transit ticketing system.

In fact, my future transport system may still include these five types, modes of transport are: railway, roadways, airways, waterways and piplelines. Also, among different includes of transport, railways are the different modes of transport, railways are the cheapest. Trains cover the distance in less time and comparatively, the fare is also less to other modes of transporation. Therefore, railways is the cheapest mode of transportation to compare ferry, water taxi , sea transport, bus, taxi, road system.

On conclusion, transport price is not the main factor to attract passegners to choose to catch. The importance to have a good public transport system in place. It may be one main factor to help the kind of public transport tool to attract passengers to choose to catch, because a good transport links can widen people's job search area and help them find employment. It can also reduce commuting times and reduce the cost of living, and high skilled workers are more likely to travel across longer distances to work, especially if they are following good job opportunities. So, future any one kind of public transportation tool service provider ought consider how to satisfy working people working time need to shorten journey time to any working places or student learning time need to shorten jounrey times to any schools as well as let they feel comfortable to sit on comfortable chairs or provide free internet service to themselves mobiles , laptops, when they are sitting down or standing up in the kind of public transport . It is the important factor to influence any kind of public transport service in success.

Future Non-Manual driving vehicle How
Influences Public Transport Tool Passenger Need

Nowadays, artifical intelligent (non-manual) driving vehicles are invented, it may be accepted to any countries families to feel comfortable to drive on roads, because any people choose to buy any kinds cars, when any people choose to buy kinds of non-manual (artificial intelligent) vehicles, they do not need to use their hands to drive cars, because artificial intelligent (robotic auto control wheels, it means that robots can help human (drivers) to control wheel to drive to avoid any cars crash occurrence on the roads more easily.

If one day, non-manual driving robotic control whoole vehicles are invented in successful, whether it will persuade many different conuntries families choose to buy non-manual (robotic auto control wheel) vehicles, then it will cause bus, tram, train, underground train, road transport need will be influenced to reduce or even if non-manula boats are invented, whether it will cause ferry sea transport needs will b influenced to reduce. Hence, future non-manual driving vehicles or bats invention whether they will influence public transport tool of road and sea transport passengers number reduces. It is one interesting question. I shall attempt to discuss as below:

In fact, non-manual vehicles are very attraction, to excite any person chooses to buy to drive, because people do not need often touch wheels and touch foots button to control cars to move often forever, when robotic can be invented to help human to control car wheel and foot button, any person only needs to sit on his/her car, then the car can move rapidly, because any drivers is lazy, he/she hopes machine can help her/him to drive car on the road safely. So, he/she can read book or listen music or eatch mobile movie to enjoy his/her entertainment when he/she is sitting on his/her car.He/she will feel more comfortable and enjoyable when robotic can help him/her to drive car. So, robotic (non -manual driving vehicle) can encourage people to choose to buy cars because any drivers won't need to drive cars, robotic can help drivers them to drive on the road easily, when global any one family can own one robotic auto control (non-manual driving) car at least, it may influence these owning non-manula diriving vehicle owners do not feel need to pay any fares to buy road public transport tools of bus ticket, train ticket, underground train ticket , tram ticket to go to anywhere. So, it seems that robotic (non-manual driving) vehicles may influence future any road transport passengers number reduces , because traditional catching any kinds of road public transport tool passengers will be influenced to choose to sit themselves auto (non-manual) driving cars to go to offices to work, parents do not need to follow their sone/daughters to sit on themselves non-manual auto driving cars to go to schools, because their sons/daughters can sit on themselves non-manual driving cars to go to schools more easily. In holidays, they can sit on themselves non-manual driving cars to go to cinemas, music halls, breachs, theaters, shopping centers, gardens different entertainment places to enjoy their any leisure safely because robotic can help them to drive their cars on roads safely.

So, it means that robotic auto control driving cars can influence global every family to feel that they do not need to catch any kinds of public transport tools, e.g. bus, train, tram, taxi underground train to go to anywhere because robotic auto driving cars can help any one, he/she does not know how to drive car to go to anywhere safely. So, future any one won't need to learn driving car skill, when he/she likes to buy one auto driving car. So, in passenger public transport need view, non-manual driving cars will influence them to feel any kinds of road public transport tools can help them to go to anywhere conveniently, because themselves non-manual driving vehicles can help them to drive cars to go to anywhere conveniently. They only need to tell robotic that where they want to go, when they sit on their non-manual driving cars, then robotic knows whether where destination, they want to go, their cars will auto move on the road immediately. It is one exciting and enjoyable ourney when the driver does not need to drive his/her car on the road. So, it seems that robotic (non-manual driving) vehicles invention may bring negative influence to any kinds of public transport tools service needs to passengers , when passengers had owned one non-manual driving car at least.

Why and how non-manual driving car owners need

raise public transport quality on travel time and fare

aspects

● How non human driving behavior can be influence by non-manual driving cars

In fact, impact of automated vehicless on travel mode preference, it can bring both trip purposes and distances aim raising need to any kinds of public transport service passegners. Because of technology penetration in the transportation system, the automated vehicle is set to be a future mode of transport, it may bring negative impact to future any kinds of public transport passengers needs, in special on the potential impact of these non-manual driving automated vehicles on travel behaior negative impact to public transport passenger behavior. Automated vehicles will influence future public transportation passengers feel it can bring more short time travel distances and short trip purposes more benefit than any kinds of public transport choices, e.g. bus, taxi, ferry, train, tram, underground tram etc. road and sea public transport tools, e.g. ferry, water taxi. It means that when future any passenger feels above these any one kind of public transport tool needs to spend longer travel time on journey distance and trip to compare future automated vehicles, then they will choose to sit on automated vehicles in preference, due to automated vehicles can help global any one person needs to go to anywhere rapidly.

So, automated vehicles may replace general traditional public transport tools in possible, when they are popular accepted in societies. On the other, instead of shortening journey travel distance time, (travel time) aspect, public transport fare, travel cost will be another influential factor to influence future public transport tool passengers to choose automated vehicles to replace to catch any kinds of public transport tools.

In fact, conventional cars and public transport s are perceivd as being the least attractive alternative in relation to in-vehicle travel time on short and long distance communting trips. So , future automated vehicle drivers (non -human driving) behaviors will be likely changed to prefer this mode for long distance leisure trips rather than short distance commuting trips by automated vehicles.

In fact, advanced technologies have revolutionized many aspects of human life, include the automated vehicle transport system. Also, transport system is one of the essential development aspect to particular , such as non-manual driving automation , vehicle aims to make trips safer, faster , more efficient, automated vehicles passengers and drivers can feel enjoyable to do themselves leisure behavior , e.g. read books, listen, music, listen mobile, watch laptop movies when any one does not need to consider whether their cars are safe to be driven , even any one needs to drive the automated car, because robotic can help them to control how to automatic drive this car on the road safely.

Robotic will bring confidence to let them feel that themselves cars are moving safely on the roads . In recent years, the concept of automated driving has been introduced as on outstanding platform for the next generation of driving systems that is expected to improve safety, traffic flows efficiency, reducing traffic jams occurrence chance, avoiding traffic accidents occurrence chance, e.g. avoid to crash any one person when he/ she is walking across road or crach any car is moving on the road easily, capacity, accessibility , and reducing congestion through the application of some technologies , such as vehicle to vehicle and vehicle to infrastructure communication.

So, future automated vechicles can have good driving facility systems to be installed in their cars, in order to raise safety, rapid driving speed level to let any one to feel , when they are sitting in their automated cars, e.g. using cameras, sensors, global positioning system adaptive cruise control, light detection and ranging, and advanced driver assistance system, automated vehicles can steer the vehicle and drive it automatically when passengers delegate control to a computer. Absolutely, ny replacing the driver role with an automated driving system , future one automated vehicle is able to totally free up passengers under automation levels.

So, unless future any kinds of public transport tools may apply automated robotic automated driven system replace the bus driver, taxi driver, train driver, tram driver, underground train driver to raise automated driving system service improvement level to let any one passengers to feel. Otherwise, when automated vehicles are popular to be accepted to buy in any one country in global. Then, global public tansport tool passegners number may be influenced to reduce when global any one family owns at least one automated vehicle at themselves homes .

In other words, automated vehicles can bring thes benefits to let global any one household family feels, future automated vehicles users , they can mostly behave like passengers inside the vehicle, which implies that they will be able to multitask and productive by allocating the travel time to do other activities, e.g. reading, eating, working, drinking, watching movies, listening musics, even sleeping. So, automated vechicles will motivate humans to change non-humanly driven behaviors from conventional humanly driven behavior. This non-humanly driven behavior may be one main factor to influence or encourage future any one kind of public transport passenger won't choose to pay fare to buy ticket to catch any one kind of public transport tool again, because non-manual driven behavior may hel many lazy people do not need to consdierate how to learn to drive cars skills to prepare pass any road test in order to earn the driving licnece to permit to drive cars forever. When automated vehiclesa re popular to be accepted to replace manual-driven cars in societies.

Hence, automated vehicles could potentially change the traditional human driven vehicle market to cause their manual driven cars sale buyers number reduces, when the automated vehicle buyers number increases, also they can chance globa public transport passengers behaviors to reduce to pay fares to catch any kinds of public transport tools when automated vechicles users may sit on themselves automated vehicles to go to anywhere in short time rapidly and safely in any countries.

On conclusion, future global public transport service competition is serious, because instead of global passengers had began to compare whether which kinds of public transport fares are cheaper, more safe, shortening journey time between leaving place and destination, more comfortable feeling, e.g. clean and comfortable chairs , mre free internet service facilities in order to make any one kind of catching public transport tool choice in preference. On the other hand, future automated vehicles number will increase when traditional manual driven car users begin to believe that automated vehicles can bring more safe , more comfortable, more fee-time using, more leisure satisfactory feeling, more than traditional manual driving cars. Then, when global any one household family had made choice to buy at least one automated vehice to replace themselves car(s) at home. When, they are habit to sit in themselves automated vehicles to go to anywhere, however, short or long trip . Consequently, global any one household family won't feel any kinds of public transport tools may bring personal economic saving cost, comfortable, enjoyable, free-time using benefit to compare themselves automated vehicles . It will cause global public transport tools passengers number will reduce , when many different kinds of home automatic vehicles are purchased to replace manual driving cars by global household automated vehicle users. So, in passegner transport tool choice psychological view, automatic vehicles will be possible to replace future public transport service tools. So, any public transport service providers can not neglect how to desing and improve their facilities , charge reasonable transport fare, provide more comfortable, and enjoyable sitting feeling , even applying automatic driving system to replace human drivers in order to attract passegners ' catching need choice more easily.

.

CHAPTER VI

The relationship between robotic invention and economic growth

Can robotic invention bring social economic growth? If it is possible that why and how robotic invention can assist any countries social economic growth? First, we need to know whether what economic growth means in order to answer this question. In macro economic view, economic growth may mean that GDP growth, employment ratio growth, job creating growth, unemployment ratio reduces, consumption growth, productive industries growth, service provision and service needs increases. So, it seems that any countries‘ social development , when it can have positive impact growth for any one of these issue. It implies that the country's economic is growing.

To discuss AI and economic growth issue, it may being these two main questions. Whether robotic invention may have direct or indirect relationship to influence any countries' economic growth? What are the main factors to cause robotics invention to bring the country's economic growth in its society?

On the first hand, some researchers believe that robotic invention may influence any countries‘ economic growth. However, otherwise, other many researchers find large and robust negative effects robots on employment and wages. They estimate what are more robot per thousand workers reduces the employment -to-population rate by between 0.18 and 0.34 percentage points, and is associated with a wage decline of between 0.25 and 0.5 percentage. Because many jobs can be replaced by robotics. So, it seems that robotics invention can reduce workers number and increasing wage level, even robotic increasing number, it can influence unemployment ratio increases to the country. But, some lecturers estimate that it can impact economic growth. They estimate that AI may deliver an additional economic output of around US$13 trillion by 2030 year, increasing global GDP by about 1.2% annually. This will mainly come from substitution of labour by automation and increased innovation in products and services.

What is the impact of robots on society? They may include this spillover, one robot per thousand workers has slightly less of an impact on the population as a whole, leading to an overall 0.2% point reduction in the

employment-to-population ratio, and reducing wages by 0.42%. Thus, adding one robot reduces employment nationwide by 3.3 workers. So, it seems that robotic number increases may influence global workers number increases many influence global workers number reduces as the same time. It can cause unemployment workers number increases in societies.
On the other side, robotic invention can increase productivity, because robots increase productivity, which means that fewer human hours are needed to produce a given output. But, higher productivity also reduces production costs and output prices. Consequently, robotic production anticipation , it can increase the quality demanded by consumers, and firms hire workers in this increased demand.
But, when robotic production participation to any industrial manufacture, it can also bring negating effects, when they are entering the workforce, e.g. higher maintenance and installation costs to factories, enhanced risk of data breach and other cybersecurity issues, reduced flexibility, anxiety and insecurity regarding the future social development. So, it seems that robotic invention can bring the future of workplace automation may reduce workers number of factories, loss of jobs and reduced employment opportunities to global future workers, potential job lose, initial investment costs to employers. However, AI may also bring harmful to our future societies because if AI surpasses humanity in general intelligence and becomes " superintelligent" , then it could become difficult or impossible for humans to control. Moreover, a second source concern is that a sudden and unexpected " intelligence explosion" might take an unprepared human race by surprise. Hence, robotic invention may become human enemy or soldier, if human applies it to social damage aspect.
However, robotic invention can also bring advantages to our future societies in possible, robotic automation may bring advantages to employers : cost effectiveness, improved quality assurance, increased productivity, avoiding workers need to work in hazardous environments. But,. AI can also bring positive impact our daily lives, such as artificial intelligence can dramatically improve the efficiencies of our workplace and can argument the work humans can do. When AI takes over repetitive or dangerous tasks, it frees up the human workforce to do work, they are better equipped for, tasks that involve creativity and empathy among others.
However, robotic invention may bring organizational benefits in our societies. Robots will have a profound effect on the workplace of the future. They will become capable of taking on multiple roles in organizations, e.g

bookkeeping or writing law draft simple clerical tasks. So, it's time for us to start thinking about the way we shall interact with our new coworkers. To be more precise, robots are expected to take over half of all low-skilled jobs in our societies, e.g. cleaning , warehouse picking up delivering tasks, restaurant cooking, hotel front line customer service, hotel room food delivery tasks etc.

So, when robots would be used in many fields all over the world. However, robots can not totally rule over the workplace by replacing all humans at jobs to keep economy afloat. Hence, robots in the workplace may bring advantages, they will not have bad emotion problems, such as safety of utilizing robotics to work in dangerous workplace. Robots do not get distracted or need to take breaks robots never need to sleep or they need to divide their attention between a multitude of things, perfection, let employees to feel happier and safe to work when robotics can help workers to work in dangerous warehouses or factories, workers can be replaced from robotics, increases productivities and job creation , even raises efficiencies in any workplaces.

In our future, whether robots won't destroy humans. It depends on how humans choose to apply this technological worker tool. A robot may not injure a human being or, though inaction, allow a human bring to come to harm. A robot must obey the orders given it by human beings, expect where such orders would conflict with the first law. A robot must protect its existence as long as such protection does not conflict with the first or second laws. How AI technology affects us in the future. They are concerned that we will see increases in stress, anxiety, and depression as digital lives expand. Meanwhile , we shall need to adapt our future digital living, there will be less face-to-face interaction , increased inactivity, poor in-person communication skills and an overall distrust among people. For robotic invention case example, future robotics can may focus on developing these five major field: Human -robotic interface, mobility, manipulation, programming, sensors and their importance to robotics development.

Robots can be applied to educational aspect. Robots can be used to bring students into the classroom that otherwise might not be able to attend. Robots such as the one mentioned are able to bring school to student who can not present physically. Simulators-high school sees the strongest example of stimulators within drivers' education courses, e.g. Google's worker robots. Google is planning to produce worker robots with personalities. So, robots can help teachers automate key classroom processes, integrate advanced technologies, acclimate students to technological change and helping identify personalized learning potential and discovering key learning trends.

- How manufacturers to raise efficiency in order to improve economic growth in possible to apply manufacturing robots to improve help economic growth

(AI) can be defined as the capability of a machine to imitate intelligent human behavior. If AI can imitate any talent humans to learn how to improve their behaviors, e.g. manufacturing industry worker behavior improves to raise GDP growth or productive number grows rapidly . Can artificial intelligence being labour to become automated? Allows an ever-in-to increasing number of tasks previously performed by human labour to become automated in the ordinary production of goods and services process.

Can (AI) create new ideas and technologies to help businessmen to solve complex problems and improve automation in the production of goods and services. The question concerns how (AI) manufacturing technology can impact economic growth?

(AI)'s new form of automation live, self-driving cars, or they may bring high levels of skill,such as legal services, radiology, and some forms of scientific lab-based research. Can it allow our societies be impacted on economic growth, due to automation to disicipline our modeling of AI.

In fact, AI automation to production of new ideas to future any industrial manufacturing process. It can influence to market structure, organization restructure, reallocation and wage inequality. So, discovering to AI automation can help future any organizations need to change existing task or discovering new tasks that can be used in production a reflects the fraction of tasks that have been automated.

It brings automating old tasks when automated could be constant, leading a stable , capital share and a stable growth rate. Hence, in long term, AI automation manufacturing technology may help businessmen to reduce large manufacturing cost in order to achieve stable micro economic benefit to them when they can apply AI automation manufacturing technologies to improve their productivities in efficient manufacturing method. For Coca Cora soft drink example, if Coca Cora applies AI automation to raise its productive soft drinks number. Then , it can manufacture many soft drinks number in short time per day. Then, its sale number can be increased, when it has enough number to supply to global to sell its soft drink. Consequently, soft drink sale number must grow rapidly significantly.

The fact that automated goods are produced with cheap capital , but it can also help business to raise production number significantly . How this superintelligence affect the economy? It seems physical tasks are essential to producing output, but when the manufacturer applies robotics to help production . Then, employees number may reduce, due to robotic participation, wages expenditure may reduce , but production number may increase .

So, AI increases the motivation at physical tasks. Hence, AI must may bring production growth innovation incentives to any manufacturers. Finally, with imitation and learning being performed mainly by super machine in developed economies. Then , research labor would become devoted to product innovations increasing product variety or inventing new products (new product lines), to replace existing products.

It is one good example to explain that how AI can bring long term social economic benefit to any manufacturers, when any old (existing) product lines are improved to innovative new product line by robotic manufacturing participation. Moreover, AI can change market structure to be reduced competition. When be escape competition effect tends to dominate at low discouragement effect may dominate for higher levels of competition or in less advanced economies. Hence , AI can also affect innovation and growth through potential effects, it might have on product market competition. So, it seems that (AI) can respond on helping social economic growth principle. On conclusion, although robotic invention may bring disadvantages to raise unemployment ratio in possible when there are many low-skilled jobs are replaced by robotics, but at the same time, robotic may be applied to education aspect, when we are experiencing digital knowledge social development stage. Hence, smart robots ought may help humans to raise economic long term growth in possible when robotics can help the developing countries to develop more rapid to be developed countries as well as they can help the developed countries to develop more advanced both in global whole one economic developed societies. So, when robots can assist any countries to cooperate together, any countries are not independent, we need robots to assist develop between countries. Then, robots can assist any countries to develop economic growth in possible in future this day comes.

How robotic helps to solve recession

Is the use of robots to job market increasing during the Great Recession? Some researchers constructed a measure of the use of robots—commonly referred to as "robot intensity"—to estimate trends in robot exposure across more than 250 metropolitan areas and over time, finding that: During the Great Recession, robot intensity plummeted. But since 2009, robot intensity has sharply increased nationwide. They felt that robots may influence recession in possible. How are robots going to affect our jobs? Most analysis tends to be prospective in nature, and estimates of future impacts on employment vary widely, with some studies predicting that as many as 50 percent of all workers are at risk of losing their jobs to automation. Even less is understood about the actual impacts of robots on jobs, wages, and workers today. If there are many low skillful jobs e.g. cleaner, warehouse deliver, cooker, restaurant waitor etc., even high skillful jobs, e.g. accountant, lawyer, doctors etc. occupations are replaced by robotics. Then, our societies will increase unemployed people number. Consequently, great recession will be caused by robotic workers because when our societies have many people lose jobs, then many people loss income, then our consumption desires may be influenced to reduce. Consequently, many businesses may lose many customers. Low consumption desires may bring serious recession to any countries, due to robotic workers number increases to replace human workers in global societies.

The reason is that new technologies of the period have enabled people to be very productive while working part-time. Businesses do not need large numbers of employees, so individuals can devote most of their waking hours to hobbies, volunteering, and community service. In conjunction with periodic work stints, they have time to pursue new skills and personal identities that are independent of their jobs. Developed countries may be on the verge of a similar transition. Robotics and machine learning have improved productivity and enhanced the economies of many nations. Artificial intelligence (AI) has advanced into finance, transportation, defense, and energy management. The internet of things (IoT) is facilitated by high-speed networks and remote sensors to connect people and businesses. In all of this, there is a possibility of a new robotic society that could improve the lives of many people, but it also encourage future businesses apply robotics to replace human workers to do many jobs in finance, transportation, defense and energy management, medical health, hotel, tourism, cinema, theatre etc. entertainment service fields. So, robotics may bring reducing cost benefits to businessmen, but they can also increase workers losing jobs number in our societies if future many businesses make decision to apply robotics to replace human workers to do any simple ot complex jobs in global job market.

A McKinsey Global Institute analysis of 750 jobs concluded that "45% of paid activities could be automated using 'currently demonstrated technologies' and . . . 60% of occupations could have 30% or more of their processes automated."[6] A more recent McKinsey report, "Jobs Lost, Jobs Gained," found that 30 percent of "work activities" could be automated by 2030 and up to 375 million workers worldwide could be affected by emerging technologies.

Researchers at the Organization for Economic Cooperation and Development (OECD) focused on "tasks" as opposed to "jobs" and found fewer job losses. Using task-related data from 32 OECD countries, they estimated that 14 percent of jobs are highly automatable and another 32 have a significant risk of automation. Although their job loss estimates are below those of other experts, they concluded that "low qualified workers are likely to bear the brunt of the adjustment costs as the automatibility of their jobs is higher compared to highly qualified workers."

reference

James Manyika, Susan Lund, Michael Chui, Macques Bughin, Jonathan Woetzel, Parul Batra, Ryan Ko, and Saurabh Sanghui, "Jobs Lost, Jobs Gained: Workforce Transitions in a Time of Automation," McKinsey Global Institute, December, 2017.

Melanie Arntz, Terry Gregory, and Ulrich Zierahn, "The Risk of Automation for Jobs in OECD Countries," Organization for Economic Cooperation and Development, Working Paper 189, 2016.

However, some economists felt opposite opinions, they believes that future many businesses won't choose whole applying robotics to replace human workers in global job market. So, they are only human workers assistant role. Economists have, on the whole, been fairly discuss about the impact of robots and AI on workers. History is strewn with incorrect predictions of the looming irrelevance of human labour. The economic statistics have yet to signal the arrival of a robot-powered job apocalypse. Outside of slumps, firms remain keen to hire humans, for example. Growth in productivity—which ought to be surging if machines are helping fewer workers produce more output—has been unimpressive. A look beneath the aggregate numbers, though, reveals that change is indeed afoot. They believes that an AI-induced change in the mix of jobs need not translate into less hiring overall. If new technologies largely assist current workers or boost productivity by enough to spark expansion, then more AI might well go hand-in-hand with more employment. This does not appear to be happening. Instead the authors find that firms with more AI-vulnerable jobs have done much less hiring on net; that was especially the case in 2014-18, when AI-related vacancies in the database surged. But the relationship between greater use of AI and reduced hiring that is present at the firm level does not show up in aggregate data, the authors note. Machines are not yet depressing labour demand across the economy as a whole. As machines become cleverer, however, that could change.

Take work by Daron Acemoglu and David Autor of the Massachusetts Institute of Technology, Jonathon Hazell of Princeton University and Pascual Restrepo of Boston University, which was presented at the recent meeting of the American Economic Association (AEA). The authors use rich data provided by Burning Glass Technologies, a software company that maintains and analyses fine-grained job information gleaned from 40,000 firms. They identify tasks and jobs in the dataset that could be done by AI today (and are therefore vulnerable to displacement). Unsurprisingly, the researchers find that businesses that are well-suited to the adoption of AI are indeed hiring people with AI expertise. Since 2010 there has been substantial growth in the number of AI-related job vacancies advertised by firms with lots of AI-vulnerable jobs. At the same time, there has been a sharp decline in these firms' demand for capabilities that compete with those of existing AI.

An AI-induced change in the mix of jobs need not translate into less hiring overall. If new technologies largely assist current workers or boost productivity by enough to spark expansion, then more AI might well go hand-in-hand with more employment. This does not appear to be happening. Instead the authors find that firms with more AI-vulnerable jobs have done much less hiring on net; that was especially the case in 2014-18, when AI-related vacancies in the database surged. But the relationship between greater use of AI and reduced hiring that is present at the firm level does not show up in aggregate data, the authors note. Machines are not yet depressing labour demand across the economy as a whole. As machines become cleverer, however, that could change.

Evidence that AI affects labour markets primarily by taking over human tasks is at odds with some earlier studies of how firms use the technology. A paper from 2019 by Timothy Bresnahan of Stanford University argues that the most valuable applications of AI have nothing to do with displacing humans. Rather, they are examples of "capital deepening", or the accumulation of more and better capital per worker, in very specific contexts, such as the matching algorithms used by Amazon and Google to offer better product recommendations and ads to users. To the extent that AI leads to disruption, it is at a "system level", says Mr Bresnahan—as Amazon's sales displace those of other firms, say.

New work by Ajay Agrawal, Joshua Gans and Avi Goldfarb of the University of Toronto suggests that this state of affairs may not persist for long, though. As the quality of AI predictions improves, they write, it becomes increasingly attractive for AI-using firms to restructure in more radical ways. At some level of accuracy, for example, Amazon's ability to predict consumers' desires could encourage the firm to adjust its business model—by pre-emptively shipping goods to consumers before they ever go searching at Amazon in the first place—in ways that are likely to change how many workers and of what sort the firm requires. In that event, the influence of AI on the economy could change dramatically. So, such as Amazon case, it applies robotics are only concentrated on predicting consumer prediction aspect, AI is only assistant role to Amazon human market researchers. They help Amazon market researchers to gather consumer behavior data , but Amazon human market researchers need to do marketing analysis tasks by themselves. So, Amazon can not employ human market reseachers jobs position in itself company. Amazon needs robotic and human market researchers to do market research tasks in order to achieve how to predict consumer behavior more accurately. Thus, it seems that future large enterprises won't fire any professional staffs more easily because some complex tasks, e.g. analysis tasks, they believe that human's analysis can make more accurate judgement to compare AI's analysis.

However, some scientists believe that some skilful professional occupations , they have possible be replaced by robotic. Will Architects and Engineers be Replaced by Robots? It's not uncommon for people to think they may be replaced by a robot in the workplace. After all, it's happened plenty of times before. For example, the rise of the mechanical assembly line saw machines replace people in the early 20th century. With recent advances in artificial intelligence (A.I.), it's entirely possible that more jobs are at risk.

Even skilled workers, such as architects, programmers and engineers may be at risk. One day, an A.I. software developer may be able to do everything that a human programmer can do.

Recent reports have not abated this thought process. In fact, the 2016 Economic Report of the President seemed to suggest that artificial intelligence is playing an increasingly important role in the engineering industry. Just think about the software you use in your work. Many software packages can handle a lot of the complex calculations for you. Yes, this cuts down on the amount of work you do. However, this automation may also present a threat to your job. What if the future sees these same software packages handling data input, as well as processing.

Automation is important. The use of artificial intelligence, alongside various other technologies, has always improved production. More work gets done, which means that businesses make more money. Architects and engineers constantly look for ways to speed up their work. The desire for automation has informed many recent software innovations. Furthermore, project methodologies, like Building Information Modelling, place automation at the fore. That's great for speed and efficiency, but what does it mean for architects and engineers? History has shown that automation has a very human effect. People lose their jobs because machines can do them faster. Just think of it from a business viewpoint. Do you want to pay 10 or more employees, or invest in one machine? More often than not, the machine will cost less than the employees, even if you factor maintenance into the equation. It's a simplification, but not an invalid one. Businesses make these sorts of decisions all the time. By pushing for automation, architects and engineers may be slowly working themselves out of their own jobs.

Several studies have also suggested that artificial intelligence may cause job losses. One recent example comes from the University of Oxford. The study found that over 700 types of jobs are at risk of technological disruption. All told, this means that about 47% percent of jobs are at risk because of artificial intelligence. That is a huge amount of people who may find themselves obsolete due to advancing technology. The same study also mentioned a concept called the "technological bottleneck". The researchers used this to determine how "at risk" a job was of displacement. The bottleneck takes three factors into account:

•How much creative intelligence the role needs

•If manual manipulation and perception is required

•The role of social intelligence in the role

If a role requires a high degree of any of those three things, it's less likely that it's at risk from artificial intelligence. Architects and engineers are a good example. These professionals require a great deal of creative intelligence. Artificial intelligence and robots may not be able to emulate that creative intelligence. As a result, it's unlikely that architects and engineers need to worry about losing their jobs. Right now, at least. The study concluded with a cautionary note. It said that just because automation enhances an architect and engineer's work right now, it doesn't mean that automation won't replace that role in the future. So, if future human architects or engineers jobs can be replaced to do by robotics. Then, robotic architects can help the architectural firms to design more attractive architectural plans to satisfy construction firms clients needs in short time or robotic engineers can help the engineering design firms to design more attractive machines to satisfy any engineeing customers needs in short time , when robotics can be invented to own excellent creative ability to compare human architects or engineers. So, these two professional occupations will be lost when robotic architects and robotic engineers can be invented to own excellent creative ability to compare human architects or engineer in future one day in possible.

However, robotic architects or engineers may bring advantages and disadvantages both aspects:

On advantages aspect:

Artificial intelligence allows us to do all of the following:

•The completion of mundane tasks that would otherwise take a lot of labour hours. Automating such tasks frees up skilled workers to work on more important tasks.

•A.I. is not as prone to making errors as a person. As long as the A.I.'s programming is good enough, you should find that calculating errors and similar issues become problems of the past.

•Speed is a key feature of artificial intelligence. Huge datasets no longer provide any problems to businesses, as automation allows for much faster processing. This means that a business can spend money elsewhere.

•The most complex A.I.s reduce the amount of risk attached to the decision-making process. The "Curiosity" Mars rover is a good example. It's programmed to choose the best course of action depending on its position.

On disadvantages aspect:

It's not all good, unfortunately. The following are some of the bad points of artificial intelligence:

•The previously mentioned job losses can cause all sorts of problems for staff morale.
•Some believe that artificial intelligence gets rid of the human element. The nightmare scenarios in films like "The Terminator" may seem far-flung, but that doesn't mean there isn't a risk in letting machines make all the decisions.
•A.I. relies on pre-existing knowledge, which means it lacks creativity. Attempting to use it for creative endeavours may result in failure.
•Algorithms may not be able to make judgement calls in disaster situations. Again, the A.I. may not take the human element into account, no matter what's actually happening on the ground.
Oe people management aspect, what do you think would be the reaction to a robot attempting to manage people? It's likely that a lot of people won't take to kindly to artificial intelligence telling them what to do. Many underestimate the importance of people skills in the architecture and engineering profession. Architects and engineers must be able to organise workloads and manage individuals. It is sure, A.I. device could handle the former. Scheduling is a task that many already automate. However, A.I. will fall down when it comes to the human relationships that are so vital in a team environment. An A.I. won't understand when somebody is demotivated, or why. It won't make allowances for the human issues that affect every problem. This makes skilled team members even more valuable. As A.I. takes an increasing role in the workplace, the need for people management will become more important. Architects and engineers with those skills may even find they make more money to employ them. Although, it is possible that AI can replace human architects or engineers to do their tasks to be better , it can help any one architectural or enginering firms to improve design performace in order to satisfy customers design demand, but our societies will increase unemployment ratio to engineers and architects number, even universities will reduce architect and engineering students number. Our traditional professional knowledge will be felt to be rubblish when these professional subjects won't be useful to help us to find jobs easily. So, AI invention will influence many students won't choose to study these two subjects. Our societies will be influence to experience knowledge recession when knowledge will become rubblish because robotics invention , it can do many human professional jobs to do. " knowledge recession" will be important factor to bring economic reccssion, because human can not be encouraged to learn any new knowledge to

prepare to enter job market due to robotic invention can replace us to do more complex tasks in our future societies.

Can robotic leadership be good solution method when recession had come to the country?

On leadership management aspect, can robots become clever leadership to any organizations? As artificial intelligence becomes further embedded into our everyday working lives, we are already seeing the footprint of machine learning, automation, algorithms and robots in many of our professions and sectors. However, when we look at the upper levels of business management and leadership, these technological shifts are less evident, with C level Executives continuing to lead and strategise as they have done before. In Ireland, there are more than 500 CEOs. The question is, when will we start to see machines and robots play a more central role in the CEO sphere, and is a 'Robot CEO' realistic in the short to medium term?

New research shows that 24% of people aged 25-29 would replace their boss with a robot, demonstrating an interesting trend among Generation Z. However, these data sets are perhaps less founded in AI and robotics and more in current employee engagement. It's telling that the 20-30% of people who would willingly replace their human boss with a robot is about the same percentage of people who are consistently classified as "actively disengaged" at work. In addition, research from analytics giant Gallup demonstrates that 70% of how we feel about work, namely our emotional commitment, is driven by who our manager is, again underlining the centrality of human behavioural traits when making decisions on leadership.

As the Irish economy moves forward, values will define how we use and leverage the potential of AI. Tomo Noda of the Harvard Business Review believes that we will need more focus on leadership with humanity, ethics and integrity, stating "only good people can create good AI."With many roadblocks and challenges for the economy looming, primarily in the shape of Brexit and trade tariffs, it is a sound integration of both human and tech which will provide the leadership required to ensure our economy remains robust. Human leaders have played a central role in helping to steer us out of the 2008 recession, and with diplomacy and relationship building key to our post-Brexit future, humans will undoubtedly be the key influencers within the C level for decades to come. Hence, it seems that future organizations ought choose to apply robots to assist leaders to do make important decision, if robotics can assist leaders to make any important decision to conclude the best results to improve any companies performance. Then, GDP may be influenced to increase or grow rapidly, when recession had come to the country. So, robotic leadership may be one solution to solve recession method in possible.

The Recession Cometh and Robots are Ready

In economic demand vs. supply theory indicates that consumer appetites for customized product and their expectations for ever-lowering costs. So the current tug-of-war over if, when, and where a recession will hit is not unchartered territory. For manufacturers, though, the uncertainty is particularly challenging, as the flexibility that allows operations to reflect the pace of the economy simply isn't there. The economy has been growing. Unemployment is down. Last year's Christmas sales were better than they've been in a long time. All good and logical reasons for manufacturers to hire.

Recently though, there have been signs that instability is coming. The US stock market experienced extreme volatility as 2018 came to a close. The Federal Reserve raised interest rates and laid down some pretty clear language that more was to come. Consumer confidence fell. In the UK, a deal on Brexit that would allow British manufacturers to continue to do business with the EU seemed elusive at best. The Chinese government announced that growth in its economy has slowed. And the "R" word started to appear with more frequency. These are not signs that inspire confidence. So, manufacturers once again find themselves in a place they know so well. The rock: the need to hire workers to keep ahead of demand. Compounding this challenge is that unemployment is low and it is very hard to find people with the skills needed to take a job in manufacturing and be ready to work on day one. The hard place: overwhelmingly, today's automation is fixed, expensive, and able to perform only a single task.

As one supply chain executive of a global automotive firm shared recently, "In a downturn...it is about flexibility. All of the automation we have cost too much and it is too complicated to change what it does. What we need is flexible automation that can respond when and how we need it to."Can robotics be applied to manufacturing industry to avoid cost reduces to manufacturers when consumption number reduces or recession is coming? So what makes the most sense? Hire, hoping that if and when recession comes, it will be short-lived and you won't have to lay folks off? Or try to invest in reconfiguring existing automation?

Hence, cobots give manufacturers the flexibility they need to thrive in good times and not-so-good times. Advances in robotic technology make it possible to put cobots to work

- at lower costs
- on more than a single task
- in the same amount of time, it takes to train a person – or even less

With collaborative robots, manufacturers can build the operations they need to compete and thrive regardless of the economic climate, where manufacturing robotic participation can help organizations to reduce labours number on strategic tasks and flexibility is part of the organizational human resource cost reducing strategy. It seems that robotic manufacturing workers can help organizations to reduce manufacturing cost when recession is coming. Consequently, these applying manufacturing robotic businesses may prolong business life time in possible. So, it seems that manufacturing robots may help organizations to reduce manufacturing cost to keep life when recession is coming.

www.ingramcontent.com/pod-product-compliance
Ingram Content Group UK Ltd.
Pitfield, Milton Keynes, MK11 3LW, UK
UKHW021923190726
13853UKWH00002B/815

9 798887 335032